T0162756

Transitions from the Sitka, Alaska Wordsmith

Book 3 of the
Martin R. Strand, Sr. Trilogy

iUniverse, Inc.
Bloomington

Transitions from the Sitka, Alaska Wordsmith
Book 3 of the Martin R. Strand, Sr. Trilogy

iUniverse books may be ordered through booksellers or by contacting:

iUniverse
1663 Liberty Drive
Bloomington, IN 47403
www.iuniverse.com
1-800-Authors (1-800-288-4677)

ISBN: 978-1-4502-8528-5 (sc)
ISBN: 978-1-4502-8529-2 (ebk)

Printed in the United States of America

iUniverse rev. date: 3/1/2011

DEDICATION

This book is written by Martin R. Strand,

a Kaagwaantaan man named K'wách

In memory of our ancestors and Tlingit elders

Kiks.ádi & Kaagwaantaan

and is lovingly dedicated to our grandchildren: Lila

Denali

Gary

Ben

Tyler

Shelby

FORWARD

Pat Sheahan

My friend Monty Wilson went to school with Martin and would almost always comment after an encounter with him, that, "he has always marched to the beat of a different drum." Martin Strand came off at first impression as peculiar. Known as Brother Martin he had a way of presenting himself at first with comedic one liners that disarmed and made new acquaintances feel comfortable. But it also made an impression that he had a silly disposition. In fact, Martin was observing and reflecting and appreciated everything and everyone around him with an astute sense, guided by the conviction that all were important, even sacred.

First impressions are often deceiving. Martin belonged to many groups and to many people. He didn't always enjoy being front and center, however. Rather, he participated in his complicated social world with the ironic eye of an outsider looking in, simultaneously showing solidarity and yet sometimes feeling himself partly outside and on the margins. It is that rare combination, albeit contradictory, that gave him that blessed gift of poetry and artistry.

As to his work, Brother Martin is significant because his words and the images he captured represent an important but confusing time for some Sitkans, especially those that are residents year round over the course of decades. I will try to explain. Martin was "old school". He belonged to the Alaska Native Brotherhood (ANB) because his grandfather's heart "bled ANB".

This group is itself an interesting combination of people, holding to tradition and embracing modern realities. Martin was a man in two worlds.

On the one hand, he was never as animated as when we went hunting and fishing in the traditional grounds around Sitka Sound. There he hunted seal and recalled trips with his family to fish camp when he was young. He took pride in his status at Dog Point Fish camp, where he had a bedroom dedicated to him for when he would come to teach any student who was interested in catching and preparing salmon. Martin taught me about marksmanship and ethics and friendship. We reloaded ammunition together and told stories and dreamed about future excursions.

What we caught, we shared. And we went to ANB meetings together. It was there that I witnessed his allegiance to his clan and to the memory of those Native peoples that had gone on before him. Martin's identity is tied to the Kaagwaantaan clan and nothing made him more proud than that affiliation.

But Martin was a Renaissance man, too. He grew up in the cottages of Sheldon Jackson College, somewhat separate from the traditional native neighborhoods of Sitka. He may have been only a mile away, but Martin would pay a price of this separation by being on the fringes socially. The reward, however, was the chance to be mobile and to expand his opportunities.

He motorcycled across Canada and the U.S. He went to the University in Ohio. He learned piano, hustled people in pool halls, took up photography. At home, Martin ventured into radio broadcasting and computers. He enjoyed bicycles and socialized in any place that might be susceptible to a story in exchange for a cup of coffee or tea. He took up the art of peacemaking and mediation.

And he watched things carefully, documenting people, times and events with an eye toward tribute, not judgment. He was as apt to quote a French philosopher as he was a Native Elder. Watching Martin watch others, I have often wondered how those seas of influence converged in his mind. I believe he used his crafts as a way of maintaining sanity and letting things stand on their own merit. And we are the recipients of his creative compartmentalizing. Creative endeavor is by nature both limiting and expressive.

Martin Strand will also be remembered for being friendly. When I had coffee with him, I was amazed at how many people he knew by first name. He related to the young person serving ice cream at McDonalds' with the same level of attention he would as someone with notoriety in town. He was gentle and saw the best in people and situations. The topics he wrote about and the subjects he photographed related to the average person in town.

And that is what made Martin so exceptional. His industry and unpretentious personality gave voice and honor to what others deemed ordinary and unworthy of celebration. We need caring people to help us see the intrinsic beauty and value of every day life. We needed Martin to be with us and yet apart so that he could respond to the cadence and syncopation of rhythms that at first seemed contradictory and tense.

We needed him to help us to stop, consider and find meaning in the routines of life. Martin marched to the beat of a different drum, but it was the cacophony of sounds that his town, state and nation provided him. Now we can reciprocate as friends do, by listening and learning from him.

AN EXPRESSION OF APPRECIATION

If Martin were writing this expression it would be as long as one of the books of the trilogy. It would include grandparents down to grandchildren, and every family person in between. It would include those whose eulogies have been presented in the third volume of the trilogy. It would include teachers, professors and students related to his formal education along with those who aided him in his cultural learning. It would include those who participated with him musically, or over a cup of coffee, or in camp activities and particularly those who aided him in his medical battles. Every fishing buddy, along with every hunting buddy along with every 'gatherer' would be included. It would include every citizen, or clan member of Sitka, a unique city located in Southeastern Alaska, the beauty of which can not be equaled. Martin was never exclusive.

As the editor I would like to thank Marcia for her long hours of search for his writings, his pictures and her holding together of the family. Our thanks is extended to James Poulson for the picture of Martin, to Henrietta VanMaanen, to Dawn McAllister, proof-reader and occasional editor, and to Dick and Judy Marcum for their technical computer skills. And I extend to God thanks for the ability to put Martin's thoughts together in these books.

Sincerely, Ken Smith, editor.

Contents

CHAPTER 1 THE GRANDCHILDREN SPEAK OUT. 1
BEN 1
TYLER 3
LILA 4
SHELBY 5
DENALI 6
GARY 7
CHAPTER 2 TESTIMONIES 9
BUZZ 9
CEMETERY VISITED 11
AN INVITATION 13
REMEMBRANCE 14
KARL & ZARA 16
MARK JACOBS 18
OUR MAN IN JUNEAU 20
MILESTONE 22
A REMEMBERING MOMENT, PHILLIP JACOBS 24
VELMA BAINES 26
REMEMBERING HERB 28
MEMORIAL DAY 2000 30
CATALINA'S SHINING FACE 32
THE BEST FRIEND OF MR. T 33
KAAGWAANTAAN REMEMBRANCE 35
THE EMPTY CHAIR AT TABLE 3 37

WHAT A RICH FULL LIFE 39
AND THE MUSIC OF HER LIFE GOES ON. 41
A YEAR IN THE OCEAN OF TEARS.. .43
ALASKA NATIVE BROTHERHOOD FOUNDING FATHERS. . . 45
PERATROVICH DAY 2005 46
HE ALWAYS DID HIS HOMEWORK. .48
TIMES OF STRUGGLE 51
"M J" REMEMBERED 53
TO REMEMBER THE SPIRIT OF JOE. 54
OUR GATHERING TODAY 56
FLORENCE DONNELLY. 58
SETTING SAIL 60
GILBERT KITKA 61
JOHN AND JOYCE MAC DONALD RECEPTION 63
VIGIL FOR VIRGIL 65
THE SPIRITED CARE GIVER. 66
WILLIAMSON FAREWELL 67
THEY ARE IN OUR MEMORY. 68
GEORGE MAX 70
ESTHER ANDERSON 72
STREET WARRIOR REMEMBERED .74
ODE TO EFFIE HOOK 76
RUTH DEMMERT. 78
CHAPTER 3 THE GREATEST NATION IS SELF EXAMI-NATION 79
EIGHTEEN GOING ON THIRTY 79
AREAS LONG GONE. 81
ATTIC TREASURES 83

A VISIT TO GRANDPA NEWELL. 85
CHRISTMAS 2003 87
CLOSING OF ANOTHER YEAR. 88
DESTINY. 90
DREAMS OF MARTIN STRAND 92
FILLING MY LIFE WITH HAPPINESS 94
DOWN BUT NOT OUT 96
FEBRUARY 20, 2008. 98
GRASPING FOR A LITTLE TRUTH IN LIFE 102
INFINITY 104
LOOKING AROUND THE CORNER AM I 106
HOT NEWS 108
LIFE OF A PHOTOGRAPHER 109
LOOKING AT MY LIFE FROM A DISTANCE. 111
MARTIN STRAND ON A COLD NIGHT 114
MY END OF THE YEAR FEARLESS INVENTORY 2005 117
MUSIC TELLS ME 119
MY REFLECTION 121
MY LIFE TODAY 123
MY LIFE A REFLECTION OF THINGS TO COME 125
MY NEW WORLD 126
MY REFLECTIONS 128
PEACE 130
MY RESOLUTIONS FOR THE YEAR 2001 132
OPENING MY WINDOW TO LET MY SOUL FLY. 134
PERFUME OF THE NIGHT 136
RESTLESSNESS RISING IN MY LIFE 138
POEMS, FISHING AND RELOADING 141
REFLECTIONS OF SHELDON JACKSON 144

RIGHTING THE WRONG 145
SAY WHAT NEEDS TO BE SAID 146
SITKA FIRE 1966 148
SALMON UPSTREAM....................................150
SOUTH EAST AREA REGIONAL HEALTH CENTER BUILDING 152
SLICES OF LIFE 154
THE SHED 156
THE CANOE I PADDLED WITH MY DOG 157
THE LINCOLN STREET SCHOOL....................................159
THERE I GO....................................161
THOUGHTS....................................163
UNCOMMON AND LOVING IT....................................165
MAUSOLEUM REVISITED....................................167
LISTENING INTO THE NIGHT 168
A KAYAK LESSON 170
THIS TREE, THIS LIFE GIVING TREE....................................172
TRAPPED INSIDE MYSELF 174
VICTORY SPEECH....................................176
CONCESSION SPEECH 177
THE BEGINNING SLOWLY BURNING 178
WHERE AM I NOW?....................................180
WRITING WITH MEANING, WOMEN 182
WHEN WILL MY LIFE RING TRUE AT LAST?....................................184
MARCH INTO THE FUTURE 186
WINTER IS FOR MEDITATION 188
ZONES AND DOGS AND PRICING 190
A LOOK INTO MYSELF 192
TRILOGY INDEX....................................199

A LAST LETTER

THE INTRODUCTION

BUILDING OF THE BOOK

Like a fish out of water I struggle to breathe the breath of purpose.
The possibility of my poetic work to reach a larger audience
Has a strangeness of feeling that it might eventually happen.
It never was my intention to put out a book of my work.
That there are so many hoops I have to jump through is confusing to me.

I can see the value in such a project for my family and friends.
I wonder what universal appeal my work could express to others?
What in my poetic attitude would others see of value?
Most of my effort is written on the same day of the event.
The writing comes easily knowing great people I know.

Being a 'memorial poet' is perhaps what I do best.
I rarely write about my own condition but feelings about others.
I am not one to think on my feet as I have to taste my words.
I get messages from my Tribal elders for reading my poems.
They seem to think I should be more spontaneous expressing myself.

In the beginning of the day I want to be original in my speaking.
The people I meet in my travels deserve something new.
I try to formulate something different in every day greetings.
"How are you?" they ask.
"Fair to poor with gusts to disgusting" is my quick reply.

A dramatic life appeals to me in meeting friends and others.
Why not add something extra special in our daily walk?
My mentors have played an important part in my life.
I will speak in colorful ways without current vulgarity,
Lots of reading sparks my communication skills.

In my formative years I excelled in speech and music.
Missionary contacts lead the way to long for excellence.
Perhaps, involvement in my church taught me to speak well.
Radio and TV work caused me to learn great habits.
It was a continuous learning journey I learned to love.

A long list of mentors paved the way to my eventual work.
Every success I had gathered much praise from my Elders.
My church, in not so subtle ways, guided me forward.
Mother Lila, highly educated, gave me the inspiration I needed.
She exposed me to the world's finest piano music.

I often think of my life as a whole city.
My precincts of thought wander down streets and alleys
Filling my mind of poetic thoughts on a daily basis.
I can scarcely leave my front door without capturing a picture.
My camera, an extension of my mind reaches outward.

There is a question about the camera images I make.
It is in an historical nature I photograph the passing scenes.
The daily changes that move from season to season thrill me.
This year, sadly, I missed the important shore bird migration.
So tuned to Nature this is part of my life style.

The poetic side of images gather in my dreams so often
In picture and word they visit my life constantly.
I often wonder if I am wordsmith or camera man.
If I am to publish my work which one will be dominant?
Can I combine the two efforts into one publication?
These are some of my thoughts flashing past my mind today.
Your help, dear reader, is much appreciated by Marcia and myself.
I have many questions about making initial efforts in this regard.
The machinery of it all attacks my mind in urgent ways.
But it is a bright ray of hope in presenting my work.

CHAPTER 1 THE GRANDCHILDREN SPEAK OUT.

BEN

My grandpa had a large influence on my life when I was young he was my best friend. He would take me everywhere with him in Sitka in my stroller which he liked to call my limousine. Later when I got older one of my earliest memories of my grandpa is when he would come to Anchorage to visit. It was like an adventure we would ride the bus all over town and visit all kinds of great places like the camera store, computer store, pawn shops and thrift stores. We would go to the park to play Frisbee, ride our bikes on the coastal trail and visit the senior center for a game of pool. We were always active and doing something when he was in town – I loved it. Later I would visit Sitka in the summer and spend all my time with grandpa. I would go over to his house and he had classical music playing loud enough to hear outside and he would always be working on something like one of his cameras or writing about what happened the day before. When I arrived he was always happy to see me and so was I. To see him. He had a lot to do with my love for electronics. I was always fascinated with all the treasurers he had in his house. Lots of camera equipment, computer equipment, recording equipment and musical instruments. He loved explaining to me how things worked leaving out no detail. While I was visiting in Sitka grandpa and I didn't waste any time, every day was an adventure. He had a spare bike for me and we would go everywhere, we would go fishing for dollies at Indian River for hours afterwards we would go to the park and play Frisbee for hours. I had so much fun as a child in Sitka with my grandpa that I would return every summer. When I got old enough to go, I would go to fish camp with him. It was a lot of fun. He taught me a lot, like how to set up a tent, sharpen a knife, start a fire and how to clean fish, sight in a gun and how to properly handle a fire arm. I loved every moment I spent with him and I will miss him very much. I wouldn't be the person I am today without him and I am proud to be his grandson. He has done so much for me during my childhood including being my best friend. I could not have asked for a better grandfather. I love you grandpa.

TYLER

Grandpa Strand was a very clever and intelligent man. I remember the last time we went up to Sitka Grandpa Strand took me fishing for the first time. We went out to a tiny stream where he knew there would be fish for the picking. We stayed out there for a couple of hours and during those couple of hours I learned how to clean a fish and get it ready for dinner. But more importantly, he taught me how to fish and why the natives would fish.

I felt like I was able to connect to him, and see the work as he did. I enjoy looking at the pictures he took and always remember how he taught me too many things to explain. I'm very lucky to have known him.

LILA

My grandpa was like a playful child. He would come home from a pool playing filled day at the senior center and whistle his way through the house. This brought much joy and music to every heart that heard. I remember the sweet afternoons when he would lounge on the couch with a newspaper to read and not a worry in mind.

When he got tired he would take long naps on the couch with his walkman lullabying him to sleep with his many favorite songs.

Grandpa lived a life of pleasing others and making all sad thought disappear. He struggled through the past years with his health. He often spent more time in a hospital bed than in front of a piano as he would have wished but he never got angry or disappointed.

Yet he still joked around and brought laughter into even the cold hospital rooms. Martin may be gone but he will always be in the hearts and souls of all the lives he's touched, including mine. He will never be lost.

SHELBY

I didn't know Grandpa Strand all that well but to me he was the camera guy. Where ever he went he always had his camera with him. I always thought that was really interesting. But another thing I learned was that he played the piano. He was very good at playing the piano, too. I remember when we lived out in Sandy that Grandpa, Tyler and I went to a Senior Center. And while we were there he played the piano. At the time I didn't know he could play the piano. So I was surprised. To me I'll always remember him as the camera, piano guy. Love

DENALI

My grandpa was a great guy and he inspired me to do music so some day I could be as good as he was. Also my grandpa always had a good attitude about everything and he always loved to make people laugh. Another reason I loved my grandpa was because he appreciated everything. I know we will all miss him but I'm sure he would want us to live life to the fullest and appreciate every day as it should be. I also know he would not want us to live in regret of things that happened in the past. We should all remember that the sun will come out tomorrow so we can all have a new beginning and new life. I'm sure I will miss him a lot but I'm not going to let it destroy my life. Sometimes I'll cry over him and sometimes I will laugh because I remembered what great times we had but I will try to think positive. That's how I will always remember my grandpa and I'll miss him a lot. But I know he's in a better place. Thank you, grandpa.

GARY

Grandpa had three Raven friends: Billy, Blacky and Ralphy. Grandpa fed the Ravens near his house. Who's going to feed them now? I wonder if Grandpa will find Ravens in Heaven . . . and maybe they don't need food in Heaven? What's grandpa going to do when everyone knows that Grandpa's favorite meal is the "next one?" I love my Grandpa and miss him terribly.

CHAPTER 2 TESTIMONIES

BUZZ

While most of us are afraid of living and scared of dying
Buzz was living a rich, full life.

He inspired us in so many varied ways.

My motorcycle days often included a stop at Buzz's Canteen.
I'd time my visits to the break time for:
Peewee James, Merle Williams, Gerald Gray and other
famous members of the "Mosquito Fleet."
I learned a lot about "Very Scary Rocks", Biorka and Low Island.
Buzz would listen intently and comment frequently
with great experience of those areas.

Salmon Derby time was especially important.
And Buzz was included on many successful trips with
his friends.
His dockside barge comments were always timely and
filled with rich humor, mostly directed at
himself.

He told me of his early life and motorcycling experience.
I was surprised when he asked to try my motorcycle.
I have a picture of him riding that cycle around the

Canteen lot behind the hospital.
He said, "Once you learn cycling you never forget."

Alexander C. Bilgewater was always a delight to hear
on the radio and Buzz got what he wanted.
I will miss this creative man who was a really great
communicator.
Although, he was visually challenged he could see with
great clarity what Life was all about.

We salute you, Buzz Matthews, for giving us a better life and
a view of what a Good Life might be.

CEMETERY VISITED

The love of their un-lived life blossoms here in the silence.
Decades alone, spirits wandering around the living.
There are still those who remember those years.
Ancient ones still here with strong memories alive.
There are those who took care of them in their last moments.

TB working its death on young and old alike.
There is sadness of the survivors weeping at the end.
We are witnesses to the horror of people a long way from home.
They are cleaning the lonely quarters in its emptiness.
Deep regret that they could not be shipped to loved ones.

People of all Nations to the North and South are here.
Their eternal sleep nearly forgotten where they are.
The winds come and go with the seasons.
The Island busy with civilization progress.
The restless sea all around them run by the tides.

A spark of remembrance glows lightly in some minds.
Thought of justice of what happened so long ago.

It takes generations to get something going.
A man with a purpose sparked with ancestral thoughts.
Building with determination Bob Sam comes forward.

A word from Elders, here a fragment of history there.
Encouragement in respectful ways guides his path.
Collective knowledge builds a path towards the Truth.
Thought heavy with lamentation drives the search.
Tribal members gather and show what they know.

Fragments of hope reach the far-flung living loved ones.

Something is being done to bring long-lost closure.
Our warrior of justice travels and sends the news.
Other Tribal members join in to help as they can.
Memorial moments build in their minds with strong remembrances.

AN INVITATION

The sixth grade class invited me to speak at my grandfather's grave site. I gave a talk and played my keyboard on a rainy day.

It's good to be with you today, grandfather, John Newell.
Elvira, who is learning and loves our culture asked me to come here.
Her class of bright eyes and minds are also gathered around this place.
When I was a young man I came here to learn poetry.
I would sit and read out loud works of famous poets.

It was a cold day in 1940 when we brought you here.
I was only 5 years old and you were my first lost relative.
I would be making many trips here in the years to come.
Tuberculosis had taken many of our friends and relatives.
I had it at the age of 3 but I survived.
Your people from Snail House in Hoonah came for the 40-day party.
It was the final grieving and celebration of your life's achievements.
Koohúk is your Tlingit name but we called you Grandpa Eesh.
Your daughter, my mother, Lila Newell Strand, is at the City cemetery.
Grandma Elsie is also there.

REMEMBRANCE

A whole culture lies here in the serenity of the forest.
They lived evolving lives in cultural clash.
Some went with imported sickness of the times.
Others were victims of the sea and its strength.
My grandfather, John Newell, left this world as an old man.

In earlier times cremation was the process after life.
Burial in the ground has its roots in Christianity.
Before earlier looting and vandalism, angel tombstones were here.
I have seen relatives come and sit by the departed quietly.
This is how I came here many times in the past.

As a youth I would come here to practice poetry in the solitude.
I saw my first snowy owl sitting on a gravestone here.
It was also a resting spot for deer on these mossy hills.
Robin and thrush nesting was common in this area.
To the West shrew colonies grew near a small stream.

It is wonderful that the young class took such an interest here.
How fitting with Memorial Day coming up fast.

In earlier times our family would visit and clean the grounds.
We are thankful to those who had the vision to help.
It is so right to honor those that have gone on ahead of us.

KARL & ZARA

He was in the quiet heart of his life when I last saw Paul at MoJo's cafe here in Sitka. Looking good and right up to date with his humor we chatted about our lives and the weird way things go wrong. I think our last meeting was in early August. The weather was most beautiful as we talked of national and regional issues. He commented about my riding a bike every day, ever much like I've seen him many times. I told him I was going to Anchorage for medical tests and he said, "Tell me about it!" He was no stranger to those tests.

Early on when he first came to town we were instant friends. His fierce protectionism for harbor people gave him a large body of followers because he could very well express their discontent. Our talks took us to MacDonald's, MoJo's, Dip 'en Sip, Highliner Coffee, Bayview Restaurant, Twin Dragon, Victoria's, Rain Country Coffee, Kettleson Memorial Library, Sheldon Jackson Library, and just on the streets.

One time in a blinding snowstorm, we talked for half-an-hour before someone said we should go inside for a warm drink. Lane 7 Snack Bar was one of our favorite places after 10 P.M. to meet with our friends. John Hallum and the late Joe Evans and I would meet at MacDonalds for hot cocoa and my favorite shamrock milk shake. He was severely saddened at the death of Joe to a heart attack. They were both sailboat owners and had a lot in common.

Both Paul and I had little difficulty meeting people. I do photography and camera repair for tourists and others. I am Kaagawaantaan (Kogwanton) from the Tlingit Tribe and half Norwegian. Paul would be my sounding board on native issues and I would call on his wisdom often. I think of him as a true "Mr. Freedom."

His life walk with us is his legacy in Sitka. Perhaps I helped him with his dealings with the City. I'm part cynic and would take the worst--case scenario, often opening myself to a tirade revealing my faults. It was good therapy for me none the less.

There are a lot of people that came close to Paul while he was with us in Sitka. Tomorrow September 11th. I am playing a meditation at the Lutheran Church for 911. It will be a C# minor Meditation I composed and I will dedicate it to Paul especially. He often came to the church with me to hear me play for tourists in the afternoon in the summer time.

Thanks for sharing your father with us Karl and Zara.

MARK JACOBS

What if the great people I've known attended Mark Jacob Jr.'s Memorial?
March 24, 2007

Heavily I looked into the mirror, my sorrow deep. I put on my best suit with a black raven sheen. The Louie Minard silver medallion Eagle sparkled wide. The half hour I spent shining my shoes flashed by. My Louis Shotridge musical attitude came easily.

What would Ralph Young do today to make a difference? My ancestors thoughts mingled in my mind for long moments. My neighbor, mentor Mark, has moved on and I swallowed hard. They are depending on me to say something today. I will speak because I love them as my own.

My mother, Lila, is here making sure my hair is just right. Grandma Elsie seriously considers the clam chowder she's making. Grandpa Ralph puts his hand on my shoulder to steady me.
My dad, John nods with the tip of his hat his approval. Sister Sofia ponders a complex score for the coming funeral.

We had no car in the family so we marched from the Cottages. John Newell was getting on but no one doubted his quick step. He would lead us on this sad day as he had done many times before. Heading to the hall we were joined by Sheldon Jackson people. The Southeast wind picks up fluffing the ladies hats.

Paul Liberty shakes my hand and I saw the sadness in his eyes. Susy James comes in with Scotty heading for the kitchen. Men in dark suits and ties near women so neatly dressed.
Mark is brought in by six men slowly and with dignity. Andrew Wanamaker with hat and Koogeinaa faces the coffin.

Dressed in blue and white the ANS comes in with somber steps. Andrew Hope comes forward and gives a respectful eulogy. He recalls in detail all of Mark's accomplishments of a lifetime. When the call for membership is given many come forward. Walter Soboleff gives a deeply moving prayer with such Tribal beauty.

In life Mark was not afraid to express his love for his people. He always spoke with roses about his wife of so many years. Their love spanned decades with family and friends. He led us in Cultural ways and promoted good living always. He is remembered for his total strength in expressing himself.

It is with tears of joy our eyes moisten and smile for Mark. Remembrance today has not diminished but has grown because of him. We gather in hope for having known him for so many years. My personal praise is for this man, this friend, and mentor. Mark Jacobs Junior's life echoes vibrantly today in our minds.

Martin R. Strand Sr.

OUR MAN IN JUNEAU

Our cultural batteries dimmed at the death of John Hope.
Realizing his mission early on he worked for us.
I had known him since my youth and admired his heritage.
He had known and respected my grandparents, Ralph and Elsie Young.
He told me many facets of their early lives.

My daughter, Martina, called me from Anchorage saddened by the news.
She knew the importance of John from her tribal work.

I was privileged to work with him in broadcasting on KIFW.
Even then he was foremost in inspiring cultural life.
I think I caught some of his positive attitudes in seeing things.

When he left Sitka we always thought of him as 'our man in Juneau.'
His vision for Tlingit and Haidas was always forward thinking.
In many Assemblies he would speak with a down-home wisdom.
He always remembered and embraced we Sitkans.
Many times he would remind us of our regional responsibilities.

He was a consensus leader in ANB taking the views of the body.

A speciality of his was listening to the Elders.
It was his wisdom to verbalize their views so all could understand.
He was sharp on the floor with options for solutions to difficult problems.
Just the right amount of humor is part of his legacy.

This Kaagwaantaan and my family will miss John Hope.
I will stand with Andy III, Gerry, Herb, Percy, Fred and their sisters in grieving the passing of John.

He has given us so much of himself while here with us.
We are all so blessed for having known he walked with us.

MILESTONE

Your journey will take you into several lifestyles along the way.
Taking good care of yourself is the most important step.
Your willingness to listen to views of others will help.
Making the good choices in your life goals you have already taken.
A lifelong goal of continual learning will feed your dream.

Caring for the welfare of your Tribe should be important.
Try using your energy as a building tool that will sustain you.
Aspire to find a vision like your grandma Ellen to guide you.
You cannot go wrong following the Hope legacy in this town.
Tap into the beautiful lives that have gone before you.

You have no idea how proud your Elders are about you.
Our thoughts are deeper than a smile or greeting.
Decades of positive imaging followed you since you were a little girl.
Your parents, grandparents, aunts, uncles and Tlingit Elders
Were pulling for your success all along the way.

It is especially fitting that you have completed this milestone in your life.
You will have many life building blocks constructed in your time.

You can call on all of us for help as your life expands.
Your great-grandparents, Andrew and Tillie would praise you.
You represent all the good goals of ANB and ANS.

Your tribal extensions stretch throughout our vast State.
You have relatives you have yet to meet in Southeast Alaska.
Margaret, Ellen, Fred, and Gerry will steer you in the right direction
To meet those who will enhance your life in many ways.
Accept our joy at your accomplishments on this special day.

A REMEMBERING MOMENT, PHILLIP JACOBS

Over fifteen years ago I was testing a new camera.
The rage of the day was a new Poloroid film just out.
It would make a negative and print at the same time!
I needed to test it out in a portrait setting.
It was a fortunate evening I invited Phillip to my house.

I had the lighting already set earlier in the evening.
He wore his favorite Greek fisherman hat, navy blue.
A jar of smoked salmon and Sailor Boy crackers we ate.
He seemed eager to have his image taken.
I took three shots and gave him the prints.

Later that evening I washed the negatives and dried them.
They showed great detail and I was extremely pleased.
The 4x5 enlarger projected a beautiful 8x10 image.
I printed on Luminos Canvas textured paper.
After drying them I was very pleased with the result.

The bearded young man image was one of my best.
My clients commented on this sparkling image.

Phillip's grandfather, Mark Jacobs Sr. I had photographed in the
1960's and he would have loved this grandson picture.
I have earlier pictures of Phillip as a child in the "Cottages."

I understand that he was a hunting partner with uncle Ernie.
His uncle was an expert shot with a Sako 222 for seal and deer.
Katlean Bay and Sandy Cove were their special hunting grounds
where he
would run into FB Anderson and myself.
Often they would share game with the Cottage people.

He leaves his favorite thousand dollar 222 Sako to his family.
The Jacobs were expert hunters not wanting to damage game.
They used small caliber rifles with a great deal of skill.
Grandpa Mark's favorite hunting gun, a Winchester model 70 22 Hornet.
Phillip loved hunting Jamboree Bay with Mark Jr.

I always thought of Phillip as a thinking man in his daily travels.
He never seemed threatened being alone in his work and play.
He had a good circle of friends and he enjoyed their company.
Sometimes I met him fishing up Indian River for trout.
Our favorite fishing spot was just above the dam.

His sister, Karen was a great motorcyclist around town.
I know the great sense of freedom in motorcycle riding.
Mark bought Phillip his first motorcycle from Triways Marina.
It takes a special, careful person to handle a bike.
Phillip and Karen were very skillful riders.

Now the road warrior rides a different destiny.
Mingling with Tlingit warriors of centuries past.
Hearing stories of bygone glory days of ancient times,
And vanished glory of fighting times.
At peace with the Tribe after a well-spent life.

Those of us left behind miss his humor and vitality.
I hope some of his artistic work lives on.
His sharpened knives carved wood into art.
The things he loved to do have a sharing element.
Our remembering of Phillip remains strong.

VELMA BAINES

Catching the Shore boat "Arrowhead" she goes to town.
Charlie Littlefield invites her aboard with his gentlemanly smile.
Seagulls hover behind the boat as they leave Sitka.
A southeasterly wind blows rain into the craft.
Two sea lions curiously swim a cautious distance.

A newly-wed Home Economics teacher joins Velma.
They engage a lively conversation as the boat rocks.
John Luke and Johnny Hope are also aboard just off work.
As they round the bend the "Lone Fisherman" passes.
Ruby Gossett sits quietly in the back of the boat.

There is talk of building a bridge to Japonski Island.
So far it is only a dream but a persistent one.
Velma busies herself preparing the salad of the day.
The handsome Louis Minard is chopping the steaks.
Matthew Williams is getting the oven ready.

The Baines children are running all over the island.
Their father is out fishing with the "Mosquito Fleet".

Joe Peterson just got his glorious new cabin cruiser.
Charcoal Island and Millerville house the people.
The motor vessel "Mt. Edgecumbe" is arriving with students.

Decades of change gradually came here.
The bridge was built to the airport, at last a reality.
The Baines family moved to their Wolff Drive home.
Velma continued her career at the hospital.
She swims today in a bright stream of praise.

This gathering of friends unite to wish her well.

She has an active life ahead of her.
We will be cheering every success along the way.
Her rich, full life speaks volumes of good.
We join her supportive family wishing every happiness.

REMEMBERING HERB

Herbert Hope was always around when I was growing up.
I've seen him with his father, Andrew and mother, Tillie.
Athletic, energetic, and a mind that always asked, "Why?"
"We are as smart as the questions we ask," Roger Lang used to say.
I remember Herb and Hilda presidents of ANB and ANS.

When ANB president, Herb served us well.
ANB and ANS membership was high at that time.
He surrounded himself with knowledgeable Tribal leaders.
He supported the ANB basketball team efforts.
Often he would suit up and carry our Spirit at the games.

"It was a strategic withdrawl from the Indian River fort,"
Herb always said relating to the 1804 Battle.
He organized a march to find the path of his Kik.sádi ancestors.
Several summers he came looking for the trail.
He taught us the urge to search our Tribal footsteps.

When he moved to Anchorage he also helped ANB there.
We would hear of his work through our extended Tribal family.

Always a contender in Grand Camp activities and politics,
Herb would rally the smaller communities from time to time.
His sense of Tribal family was exemplary.

I remember him most for his considerable involvement in
Tlingit and Haida Indian Tribes of Alaska.
Stinging questions about our budget and policies.
A deep sense of caring which we would have difficulty
Expressing came easy to Herb.

As leader of his delegation, be it Tlingit and Haida or ANB

Herb gave it focused attention.
This is an historically positive trait of the long line of Hopes.
I have always appreciated this leadership factory
that has served us well over the decades.

We gather in sadness today to honor our departed brother.
The grief of one family is deep, so close to the death of Johnny.
In our grief we also celebrate the enormous contribution
Herb Hope has had on our Sitka lives.
A great Alaskan who has warmed our hearts many times.

MEMORIAL DAY 2000

My brother, John Bashore, rests here for over 20 years.
As an Army soldier in World War II Occupational Forces he saw what war
Could do to Europe torn, and damaged heavily.
He never talked much about what really happened but it was a hard time.
He took comfort in the American Legion with his buddies.

He attended Sheldon Jackson and answered the call to serve.
He was a splendid athlete and outdoors man.
He would go on hunting parties and bring game to the SJS kitchen.
He and his friends would run up Gavin Hill, then behind
The three Sisters and Arrowhead, then Verstovia just for practice.

All his outdoor skills were put to task in the Army.
He was always an excellent rifleman and took Expert Marksman awards.
He trained well and was a team player for his unit.
When he returned home he joined our Forest Service and did well.
Of course, it was work in the field he loved.

He took pride in the Service and Memorial days were special to him.
The reason he's buried here is because of a tragic house fire.

Since that time we remember him on this special day.
I have photographed Memorial Day parades in his memory.
Throughout my life I've heard great speeches here, like today.

The heavy sadness of Chaplains telling of last rites.
Generals lamenting the heavy losses under their command.
Close buddies relating their last moments before death.
Collateral damage to citizens caught in the wrong time.

The Crowd full of tears gather around this place.

I did not have the opportunity to serve but I would have if called.
I believe Freedom is worthwhile and risks must be taken for it.
So I listen to the prayers for those who sacrificed their lives for us.
Respectfully I march for them and remove my hat in honoring them.
And most of all I remember, I remember - - - -

CATALINA'S SHINING FACE

I planted a beautiful seed in the mind of someone.
They saw my written word in the paper and loved it.
Our first meeting we made a close connection.
She was working at the time but radiated a breathless charm.
How could this happen in such a short time?

She spoke of a dark side of her life that is over.
What forgotten arrow pierced her soul?
A strong sadness emerged as she talked to me.
The sun warmed our thoughts as we spoke.
We were led forward in our thinking by the sea.

In the loveliness of the moment Catalina glowed.
I do not see her past, but her glowing future here.
She is so natural in her loving work.
Caring for elderly people every working day.
People sparkle just because of her being there.

I would imagine she dances her folk songs from home.
I could see her in colorful traditional dress.
Most likely she had relatives living in town,
Very much as I have extended Tlingit tribal family.
What a great day this has been for me!

THE BEST FRIEND OF MR. T

The furry little body jumped with joy after a good meal.
It was now time for the favorite walk around town.
You could tell there was great pleasure as Danny got ready.
There was extra slack in the leash for the day.
What freedom awaits Mr. T as Danny opened the door.

There is a special connection good people have with their pets.
The extra dimension a pet gives to the lives of those around it.
Mr. T is living a rich full life with the Thomas family.
The spirit of Danny is still very much alive to its life.
Does Mr. T realize yet what has happened?

Danny has always been a true Sitka Gentleman.
I've enjoyed his company at many a Senior Center lunch.
I remember the joy he expressed with his new gold bracelet.
The Eagle and Raven with the cross of his faith are shown.
He beamed with pride the day he received it and shared it with us.

He always showed up in the hot spots for hunting and fishing.
His boat, in tip--top shape, would make a grand entrance.

Redoubt Bay with sockeye, Dorothy Narrows with "Mosquito Fleet,"
The Magoons for coho are some of the places Danny would be.
An expert shot, we'd see him in the Fall deer hunting.

The Bill Thomas family are hard working people.
They had the strength to work long hours at the Cold Storage.
Skillfully chopping halibut heads and moving heavy fish all day.
Filling thousands of wooden barrels of fish salted and headed south.
Danny was a very real part of the heavy work of the times.

Their women brought skills to the Cold Storage also.

Whatever the seasons brought they were there with their men.
King salmon, herring, black cod and other fish processed.
Beautiful children were born into the Thomas family.
Today a huge legacy lives on in their varied lives.

Today we so honor the memory of Danny Thomas the man.
A generous person who cared so much about others around him.
His church experience was so much a part of his life.
A shining example of what one could do with his life.
In our grief we also celebrate the lessons he's given us.

KAAGWAANTAAN REMEMBRANCE

The feelings of grief today are the same as at the death of my grandmother,
Elsie Newell Young.
Later I was here at the passing of my mother, Lila Newell Strand.
I felt the loss at the passing of the tribal great woman, Flora Williams.
One of the Pillars of our church was Jessie Price, a great tribal loss.
And now, Lila Kirkman, Kaagwaantaan, is among them.

We follow these women by their tribal names we are given.
They shared the power and spark that Tlingit women have known through history.
Lila takes her place in history as a tribal mentor to many of us, myself included.
Over the years we have taken her to lunch.
To inquire about our Tlingit heritage.
Always willing to share, Lila gave me details about my family history in decades past.
She filled in the space about my grandfather John Newell from Hoonah's "Snail House."
Grandma Elsie's connection to Killisno was revealed.

Throughout my schooling my sister, Sofia and I were close to the Kirkmans in our grades.
Something of an extended family is how we thought of them.
My father, John Strand, fished and trapped with Lila's husband, Ted Kirkman, many times living off the land and caring for their families.

I was honored to have lunch at the senior center for over two years which Lila attended. Sometimes I tried to disguise my voice but Lila would say, "Is that you, Martin?" We would talk of better times and laugh with inside jokes.

It's been my pleasure to be a friend of this fine family for so many years.

--THE "NEWELL" LADIES
--LILA, ELSIE (mother), HARRIET
--ABOUT 1912 IN SITKA

THE EMPTY CHAIR AT TABLE 3

For all the talk centered around early Sitka.
Teddy was supreme as a fascinating intellect.
He could recall details and names the rest of us had long forgotten.
He had a way with words and played with words.
In an entertaining way he had a sense of STYLE!

From the early days of his work with Reliable Transfer
To his Alaska Lumber Pulp involvement he had a story to tell.
Catching red coho in Swan Lake creek in those glory days.
World War II along the shores of Indian River.
Teddy was there and remembered it all as yesterday.

The Sawmill Creek Dairy with steelhead running up stream.
Along with good rainbow trout fishing before the dam.
He spoke with pride of our early Sitka Scene.
Through the fog of memory Teddy would recall
Details that brought back pleasant memories.

His grasp of history reached way back in World War II.
The military was here in force in the 1940's

We talked of Army radio station WVCX and its effect on the town.
I remember going out to the station in a covered shore boat.
Military--stand up comedians entertained us all.

As I walked up to the Senior Center, Teddy would wave to me.
Table 3 would have Al Gray, Franklin James, Jacob Hemmnes and Teddy.
We had comments about the Iraq war to lutefisk at Christmas.
Clarence Dull would liven up the table from time to time.
His strong tenor voice spoke with conviction to us.

Teddy and I talked about how wonderful it would be with a pool table.
We had fun filling out those forms every three months.
You know the one that asks, "What is your favorite meal?"
I would always answer, "My next one."
That was a real knee-slapper to Teddy and the gang.

WHAT A RICH FULL LIFE

He was one of those who inspired me to look deeply into my life.
He who with a rich, full life shared the map of his life.
Like a musical score rich with detail he would recall things long ago.
"How do you know these thing?" I would ask.
Louis would say, "I was there!"

We would drive on a Sunday afternoon deep into the countryside.
A great time for reflection for the passing parade.
He hunted, fished, and gathered food for himself and family.
As a young man he was given a small open wood canoe.
Many times leaving Kake for a day of adventure.

My Elder and mentor would read my public smiles and private tears.
It was such a privilege to have him for a friend to lean on.
Always willing to help whenever he could, the day seemed brighter.
He carried the deep respect of the Tribe and wore it proudly.
Such positive attitudes grew out of this friendship over the years.

In the beginning of his carving days I was thrilled to photograph his work.
He'd let me take his bracelets home to work on for the day.

I felt like a diamond broker photographing a treasure for a short time.
As he produced medallions, rings, and necklaces I marveled at the quality.
I would come to the Cultural Center and leave very much refreshed.

Ever keeping his mind active, he learned and loved photography.
I advised him about the best equipment and he learned quickly.
We'd photograph sea lions in the harbor and the herring season.
The brilliant turning-red sockeye at Bear Cove was our favorite.
There were images of migrating shore birds in the park each Spring.

We had breakfast at Dockside, Sitka Café, Moy's Café and Victoria's.
It was there we met our Tribal extensions and renewed friendships.
In herring times we met Frank Hayward, Sr. many seasons.
We gathered around Frank Mercer, the great humorist.
My Angoon and Hoonah relatives met with Louis and me.

The lessons I learned have made me more caring and compassionate.
The kindness and generosity Louis gave I could never repay.
But I can from this day forward carry his high spirit.
I am only one of the many who Louis has led the way.
We marvel at the beauty of his life that has affected us all.

AND THE MUSIC OF HER LIFE GOES ON

I would imagine there was many a tear-soaked pillow at her passing.
A sense of shock echoed through out our God-loving community.
Our support of the family sometimes never seems enough.
The loss was so deep in many ways we cannot understand.
Our memories of Karen are so strong and will not be forgotten.

The lives of the "Cottage People" quickened at the birth of Karen.
Mark Sr. and Annie's heart swelled with pride and joy.
The hope of their lives centered around this amazing princess.
Her entire existence was to be beautifully blessed by all.
Here was a daughter that would lead the Tribe upward.

Chewing on the finest dried herring eggs this girl grew rapidly.
A blueberry and salmon berry picker helped her mother.
The alert, tree climbing darling surrounded by aunts and uncles
Was so favored wherever she went in the "Cottages."
Dad and his brothers brought clams, deer, and seal up the beach.

She had a musical heart beating a rhythm of Tribal drums.
The best teachers of the day Edith Latta and Kerry Munro taught piano.

Our young lady quickly showed her sensitivity and musical strength.
Soon she joined the high school band and fit in nicely.
Being a musical team player was part of her greater plan.

Karen's ever-widening world would soon discover the freedom
Of motorcycles and she learned how to safely handle them.
I would see her on my motorcycle rounds around town.
"You need more air in your back tire" I would say.
Days later she stopped me and said, "Your left blinker is dead."

She wore well the independence one receives by cycling.
A road warrior this beautiful, helmeted angel passed me by.
Ring ding, ding, ding, ring, ding, ding down life's highway.
Off on some distant goal for the day she'd disappear down the road.
Her motor tuned to perfection, never missing a beat!

There was a public-spirited side of Karen with her involvement in band.
During Alaska Days she took part in Cultural fashion shows.
She then joined the work force and I saw her in Anchorage Law offices.
My daughter, Martina, was one of her friends up there.
She was good at what she did as a dependable worker.

Her Elders would smile proudly at every success in her path.
The beauty of her life was from the inside to the outside.
Her mother and father were the most excellent role models.
She stopped to talk to me at Highliner Coffee in the mornings.
Bright and cheerful without complaint, I remember Karen.

A YEAR IN THE OCEAN OF TEARS.

A year in the ocean of tears with so many passing.
It seems the grieving will never stop in so many ways.
Our heavy hearts beat with sadness for our losses.
Our leader fresh in our memories is not distant.
We tried to be brave for his family but the tears came.

The many others gone is heavy on our minds.
We are thankful for the richness they gave our lives.
We gather our children close clutching our future.
We tell them the truth about the departed,
And the beacon of light that shows us The Way.

We who have witnessed so much grieving this year
Tonight light a candle of remembrance and hope.
A circle of light shines bright as we see our faces.
Our thoughts reach to the heavens. We are not alone.
The gathering tonight is a powerful side of life.

My tribal extensions breathe full of beauty.
Our meaning of life is shared in many ways.

Spiritual food rises from the fire upward.
Our grieving is lightened in this shared gathering.
We leave this church to start life anew.

Ralph Young

ALASKA NATIVE BROTHERHOOD FOUNDING FATHERS.

Organized 1912 in Sitka AK

Peter Simpson, Sitka
Ralph Young, Sitka
Chester Worthington, Wrangell
James C. Johnson, Klawock
Paul Liberty, Sitka
Seward Kunz, Juneau
Frank Mercer, Juneau
Frank Price, Sitka
George Field, Klawock
Eli Katanook, Angoon
James Watson, Juneau
William Hobson, Angoon
Marie Orson, Sec

Martin R. Strand Sr.

PERATROVICH DAY 2005

The lady we celebrate today walked among us questioning justice.
She carried the destiny of our people with precious dignity.
She listened closely to the Elders of the communities.
She and her husband were well traveled in this area.
They took frequent visits to the Cottages of Sheldon Jackson.

I was at the age of 10 when they visited our home.
There was a powerful specialness about them.
My grandfather, Ralph and grandmother Elsie greeted them warmly.
Great moments were had at the ANB and ANS meetings.
Elizabeth and Roy worked hard for our people.

My sister and I sat at the top of the stairs listening into the night.
Native leaders talked of giving us a fair chance at life.
There was singing and my mother played the piano in the parlor.
She also brought us crackers and smoked salmon.
Talking deep into the night of Native issues continued.

Hope, Jacobs, Wanamaker, Young, Simpson, Willard, Williams,
Paul brothers, Kitka and others gathered with Roy and

Elizabeth Peratrovich downstairs in our house on Kelly Street.
Discussing pending ANB/ANS Grand Camp action was foremost.
My sister Sofia and I felt something good was happening.

The talk was about the children growing up in this setting.
Grandparent concern ran heavily about a good education.
They wanted us to be at home in the new world.
They wanted our culture to survive in many positive ways.
They knew what it meant to struggle on our behalf.

Gathering here today we reaffirm our belief in their quest.

All the good that happened in 1945 for our people lives today.
Another beginning for our lives in the most positive way.
It is true that change came slowly but yet surely.
It opened doors and expanded our living broadly.

Although the work continues we have made forward progress.
Many people behind the scenes helped Elizabeth and Roy
Forge ahead to a new understanding of our lives.
We celebrate their success on this special day.
We are glad to share this day with our friends.

Martin R. Strand Sr.

HE ALWAYS DID HIS HOMEWORK

Many times I walked to the foot of Kelly Street seeking help.
A man came to the door and with a few assuring words sent me on my way.
Those few words gave me an inspiration to run for office.
They opened the door to new technical Indian Political insights.
They gave me courage to go down difficult paths.

He had a gift giving advice heavy with rich detail in his speeches.
We marveled at the familiarity he had for Tribal history.
Deep into his elderly years he gathered cultural food in Nature.
He always protected our right to live off the land.
He spoke eloquently to local, state and Federal issues.

I had the honor to be a fellow delegate with Mark Jacobs Jr.
We were with the Sitka Community Association, the
Tlingit and Haida Local Council, and the Alaska Native Brotherhood.
Most of the time he was Chairman, making sure we followed
Proper rules of order and making our meetings exciting.

There is an emptiness in our lives today at his passing.
My mentor, my help in troubled times is not here.

This tribal pathfinder reached deep into our community.
His concern for all of us was part of his outstanding agenda.
Today I honor his life force in strong remembrance.

His intense concern for our customary and traditional lifestyle
Was an important component to his work.
When some important issue came up suddenly he was there.
We were so proud that he was prepared and did his homework.
Many of those times he was our sole representative speaker.

Mark's life was not without humor.
At conventions around our area he often told knee--slapping jokes.
He was great at breaking up dignified, serious moments with laughter.
Mark Sr. also had this gift and I am happy Harold follows this tradition.
Sometimes it is wise not to take one's self too seriously.

The Jacobs family was our next door neighbor in the Cottages.
We grew up with Mark, Harvey, Ernie, Rosy and Franklin, my buddy.
Their parents Mark Sr. and Annie often visited our house.
We shared a common smokehouse in the back-yard and used it often.
Boiled dry fish with potatoes always created an enthusiastic following.

At our meetings Mark often was asked to give a prayer, now and then.
They were always timely and full of compassion for our people.
He was a strong family man and supported his church at every opportunity.
We will miss his presence in the void he leaves.
But we are glad that he walked with us in life's journey.

TIMES OF STRUGGLE

We are no strangers to times of struggle.
The vision of our Founders paved the way for our success.
We were too young to understand the fight that was building.
Our Elders' keen minds and strong resolve led the way.
Decades ago the light of freedom was dim, yet growing.

I see the moonlight tonight.
I look for the sunshine.
I feel, sadly, the darkness.

A night time with bursts of light full of hate and horrible sound.
At Memphis 1968 speeds a bullet across the way.
I read the news fresh off the teletype to the radio crowd,
Realizing we have lost a National hero for freedom
And a wave of terror washes across our land.

I see the moonlight tonight.
I look for the sunshine.
I feel, sadly, the darkness.

Martin Luther King is gone and Sitka grieves as the others.
We remember the fight he fought to lead us to the light.
Our Native Elders saw the commonality of his struggle.
Alaska Native Brotherhood and Sisterhood wept on that day.
We, too, had gone through the dark side of prejudice.

I see the moonlight tonight.
I look for the sunshine.
I feel, sadly, this darkness.

My Sitka grandparents fought for a better life for us.
Ralph and Elsie Young walked hand in hand to ANB and ANS

Each Monday night building a life for the grandchildren.
Our Founders were wise enough to capture that vision.
I am a direct product of their worthwhile effort.

There is a new emptiness in our lives today.
My mentor, my help in troubled times has gone.
Mark Jacobs Jr. our Tlingit pathfinder left us this week.
Today I honor his life force in strong remembrance.
He walked with us in truth and confidence.

"M J" REMEMBERED

Bright spirited always a ready smile for all of us
scooting here and there with confidence.
Daring of a dirt bike rider
she skirts the gravel of the back lot.

We are the bright stream of friends. She enjoyed and shared her life.
The power lunch table will miss her.
Or, the meaningful conversations and meals.
She was always concerned with "how's your day?"

With us at concerts, parades, and events,
Eyes sparkling with joy just being with us.
We would gather around her happy nature.
Rain or shine she made her way to us. Like Alice she rode in all weather.

To us she seemed to find happiness everywhere.
And her attitude carried us with her.
On my 60th year she was lunching here.
And the years followed the years to today.
We remember M J, smiling to us.

Martin R. Strand Sr.

TO REMEMBER THE SPIRIT OF JOE

His passion was complete wherever he picked up his cue.
We got the impression that it was more than just a game.
It was a total statement in the direction of excellence.
Playing flat out with all his energy was his only way.
His happiness was complete with a table run.

The attitude above was also how he viewed his life.
An expert hunter and fisher was an important part of his being.
Attention to detail in Contract Health rounded out his life.
The most important part of him was his love of people.
He had an overriding concern for the welfare of the Tribe.

My visits with Joe were decades long and meaningful.
We enjoyed our company in our games and pursuits.
He was a conservative leader in our local and regional areas.
We listened to his warnings about excessive spending in ANB,
All framed in his quiet, kind and caring pleading voice.

I can remember his insistence that his pool team practice.
He constantly reminded us that we are a TEAM.

A team works for the greater good in small and larger ways.
A team should work and learn together was what he taught.
This attitude prevailed on and off the pool table.

A founding member of the famed "Mosquito Fleet" fishing club.
The "weekend warriors" fished close to shore where trollers feared.
After a day of regular work they took to their boats for salmon.
The successful small boats brought in their share of the harvest.
They often traveled together to other Southeast ports.

Joe always took people out fishing in the many Salmon Derbies.

He generously gassed up the boat and provided the food.
All the maintenance was done well in advance of the Derby.
His guests often got good fish to enter and so did Joe.
On the slower days we played poker aboard ship.

Proudly we marched with the veterans November 11th.
We marched honoring Elizabeth Peratrovich's speech to the legislature.
Memorial Day we marched to the National cemetery.
Joe was by our side at all of these patriotic events.
Wearing his ANB hat and his clan vest Joe was there for us.

The Sitka camp was honored to campaign for Joe for one
Of the Vice Presidents of Tlingit and Haida Central Council.
During those years he served us well and kept us informed.
He was always willing to share what was going on at Tlingit and Haida.
He was a willing contributor in our Tribal concerns.

We miss him in all these pursuits that he carried on so well.
In work or play, his passion for excellence is how he was defined.
He deeply touched the lives of those in this region.
A regular part of our downtown scene he was always welcomed.
Being so well known around town was one of his high points.

Joseph Peterson, with all our appreciation, meant a lot to us.
Our public smiles and our private tears he understood.
He was quick to help in any way he could and often did.
We celebrate the rich memories he left us all.
We thank him again and again for his rich life he gave us.

Martin R. Strand Sr.

OUR GATHERING TODAY

This poem was presented at the ANB and ANS Convention meeting in Juneau at the Northern Light Church on Wednesday October 5th 2005 along with piano composition "C# Minor Meditation" by Martin R. Strand

Thinking of the spirit of grandmother and mother
Grandma Elsie and mother Lila brings to my mind reverence.
It is the music of their lives that is with me still.
I remember the humming in the kitchen preparing dinner.
The hymns came alive with praise in our church.

Since music is my most spiritual side I listen.
Uplifting concert music with great depth moves me.
I imagine the lives of those departed come alive again.
I am connected to the richness of a minor key.
As if they are giving me advice from afar.

The piano was the first Western influence in my family.
It came as a gift from our Sheldon Jackson teachers.
A whole world of expression was opened to us.
We embraced all that good music gave.
I am a product of those beginning musical times.

Another year of grieving is upon us today.
Family and loved ones have entered that deep sleep.
Our music takes a somber, reflective tone of sadness.
We gather closer together seeking answers in our pain.
Our church is here and our Elders speak to us.

The best of our Tribal ways hold up our lives.
The beauty of expression lifts our weary hearts.
We sing and beat the drum as in ancient days.

Forever seeking answers and yet so many questions.
We love and hug each other for another day.

FLORENCE DONNELLY

Her walk through life lifts our spirits to new levels. We are carried upward in inspiration for her caring ways. She is the connection to our campus mission deep into the past. The depth of feeling in her smile radiates through the room. Continuance as that river that flows by us, her music is there.

Her 9th decade has not diminished her bubbling enthusiasm. We ride with her moment to moment in fascination. Saturday is a big day for buying recycled treasures. They live handsomely off what others have cast aside. The garage sales and thrifts are also about meeting friends. Coming to Sitka and Sheldon Jackson as a young girl, learning doors were opened wide with missionary help. Isabella Bourhill, of Stevenson Hall was Florence's supervisor. Jessie Weir Price was Home Economics teacher for her. The school continues to be helpful to thousands of us.

On a gray day we students would wander over to the student store. It was a small military building from World War II, taken from the islands after the war. I would buy a candy bar from Florence. There was a warmth in her voice and she'd ask, "How are your grades coming?" "Shouldn't you be in study hall?" "I hope I'll see you in church this Sunday." "We have a game tonight and we need your cheer." We had our own on-campus therapist pushing us to be our best.

I often wonder if she took piano lessons from Dorothy Stuart. Music was a big part of teaching at the early SJS. The Sheldon Jackson Orchestra had its start in 1923. The Sitka Cottage Band was in full operation at that time. Tlingits, Haidas, and other native groups were quite musical. It was a rare night when I did not see Florence at a school game. The loudest cheers always came from her section. Husband Harold, then son Bunny, were great sportsmen on the floor.

Competitive basketball had evolved to a high level. Sheldon Jackson school played a dominant part in the region.

She walked from decade to decade meeting each challenge. Sheldon Jackson in World War II saw changes in Sitka. Destroyers and amphibian planes in Sitka Sound. Our first Military radio station was out in the islands. We all took a shore boat to visit WVCX under tight security. She sang with feeling at our Native church on campus. Her church was an important part of her life. The beauty of the choir brightened hearts at SJS. Christmas and Easter concerts had a special place in the community. Many times the Orthodox choir would join us.

This is the most special night honoring her 90th year. We gather in celebration with her and her family tonight. We take a walk through Sheldon Jackson's history. Florence continues to walk with us on this 90th birthday. We are thankful for having a part in this moment of joy.

SETTING SAIL

The music fills the emptiness of my mind tonight.
We had in depth talks as gentlemen would.
The setting, Victoria's with heavy rain beating the pavement.
We talked about what's going right with our lives.
Intelligent talk full of dreams of the dreamer.

I had the feeling that he knew the sea well.
The boat was an extension of his future hope.
He was heading North to prepare for the journey.
I was filled with envy at his sense of adventure.
Still we talked at length of the beauty of the sea.

Mike Price grew into a close friend of mine.
I spoke of touring Canada by motorcycle in the 70's.
Kayaking the waters, fishing and hunting along the way.
Our cups were filled constantly by beautiful help.
He was a good listener and a great story teller.

The Chopin I'm listening to takes a sad turn.
It speaks of trouble and hard times like today.

Then it celebrates an uplifted life all its own.
I lift a cup of coffee in praise of Mike's life.
I have learned so much, very much in his memory.

GILBERT KITKA

He lost his life in the waters off Kruzof Island. He was one of my closest friends. I presented this at his memorial service.

Our young lives crossed daily in "Cottages" for decades.
Growing up in small steps and each one an inspiration.
It was everything boys ever wanted, endless activity.
Each day was bound for adventure of one kind or another.
We had the sea, the trees, the river to explore.

Our beginning crude rafts out in the Totem park breakers.
The salt sea spray from our splashing paddles wet our faces.
Salmon swiftly scurry under our raft to security.
We watched the warships and planes out in the bay.
The high tree above the Manse was our lookout.

Gilbert and I enjoyed our company in many ways.
Slingshot hunting for shore birds was our favorite.
Cooked on the beach with salt, pepper, and butter.
Black Turnstones flew in huge flocks ripe for the slingshot.
Casting from the rocks we caught Fall coho by SJS.

In the woods above Mark Jacob's house we had our swing.
"Cottage" children had endless fun on that big swing.
I visited the place last week and the big tree was gone.
Perhaps lost in a fall or winter storm that brought it down.
I stood in the silence remembering those happy times.

We often walked to school along Crescent Beach together.
Huge piles of sawdust brought insects for the shorebirds to eat.
Smoke from the Columbia Lumber drifted low toward us.
Coho jumping along the way on their way to Swan Lake creek.
The cry of Old Squaw ducks echoed through out the Sound.

Soon Gilbert was working at Mt. Edgecumbe.
An active "Mosquito Fleet" fisherman after work,
He fished the area successfully with his working buddies.
They were the elite shallow water fishers of the time.
He found time to volunteer with the island fire department.

The Cold Storage fire of 1973 burned rapidly on that clear day.
I was busy photographing it from many angles.
I was on a boat when the ladder collapsed and got the picture.
The injured were in intensive care for a long while.

I learned my pictures were a help in insurance matters.

Today I remember my close friend Gilbert Kitka.
I consider my time with him part of the formation of my lifestyle.
His ready smile stays with me still and I see it in his children.
Our fishing stories on Indian River run over and over in my mind.
The good thoughts of our lives continue to inspire my life.

JOHN AND JOYCE MAC DONALD RECEPTION

Frequent visits to the radio station with John and Joyce.
One special day I photographed their wedding there.
Their good humor and caring lives reach all the way to today.
Their sparkle for life is just as bright as the day I met them.
However, "From this valley they say you are leaving."

I have a Christmas photograph of their first business downtown.
The business posed for me way after midnight on a snowy evening.
The window festooned in Christmas glory and full of color.
I did my best work for friends over the years.
Soon my daughter Sara Joy was happily working for them.

Our summer Music Festival always included Joyce and John.
The musicians were treated royally after the concerts.
In my visits to their home I played my latest compositions.
It was there I first had the ideas for my C# minor Meditation.
Their grand piano musically spoke to me with new ideas.

Their 25th was celebrated with Episcopalian delight on this location.
I gladly came back from Anchorage to photograph this honor.

These lifelong friends came through with generosity and caring.
"His Majesty (John), her Ladyship (Joyce) and Princess (Moira)"
Posed with royal expressions befitting their station.

I once invited them to come to my concert at the Lutheran Church.
In the music loft sat the ancient organ, piano, and synthesizer.
I played the organ and piano then moved to my true love,
The synthesizer in the choir mode as we ended the music.
People were congratulating John and Joyce for their singing.

There is beauty in their lives that they have given us.
The open road of adventure beckons them on.
We will attempt to fill the void they leave us, but not well.
We hope they will visit us often in the coming years.
Today I stand in praise of the MacDonalds this day and onward.

VIGIL FOR VIRGIL

In the quiet of this evening I listen to Schumann's chamber music.
Remembering the life of Virgil our friend of many months.
Our faithful driver Paul brought Virgil to our table.
We called him "chairman of the board" and we meant it.
He added an extra dimension to our day and that we miss dearly.

I was sad to hear of his passing while I was in Anchorage.
There was always a special place in our lives when he came to lunch.
His two harmonicas at the ready entertained and thrilled us all.
Sue the piano player inspired him to bring out the musical best.
We looked forward to those Wednesdays when they performed.

I call him my Norwegian brother in sharing our life's experiences.
He recalled many times my grandson Gary playing with Alex.
The pride he had for his grandson mirrored my own thoughts.
We seemed to be reaching out to the future life's best wishes.
He would say occasionally, "I'm well enough to take nourishment."

Jacob, Al, Cleoria, Clarence and myself on table two enjoyed Virgil.
Clarence would set the conversation tone and we all pitched in.

Virgil had several humorous stories and ready wit that delighted us.
He was our senior statesman of what an elderly person should be.
Never a complaint about health was heard while he was here.

People from the Center of the Community cheerfully brought him here.
He always had a cheerful greeting for us and called us by name.
In a sense we felt something special in the way he regarded us.
In our grieving we still celebrate the contributions of his spirited life.
He had a beauty and sense of style that we will surely miss.

THE SPIRITED CARE GIVER

In the depth of my precincts of thought and thoughtfulness I rise.
Looking at a life rich in service to others, I see Ken.
We've stood together at ANB/ANS Grand Camp many times.
At gatherings of Tlingit & Haida Central Council, Ken
In the sunshine of his life, he gladly shared his concerns.

He walked with us in our sorrow and cheered our victories.
Familiar with the cutting edge of technology he presented
The important issues of the day for our consideration.
His sound and visual forces combined with our People.
Deepening our understanding of health care was his priority.

He left open a door for my own memorial moments.
The SEARHC Memorial service was therapy for my life.
My keyboard music in the stairwell did wonders
In remembering my family that walked in life here.
So thankful am I to have this part of the remembrance.

Perhaps his greatest treasure is that he took time to listen to us.
There always seemed to be time for friendly dialogue.
His visits to this hall were frequent and I think fruitful.
We grieve with his family at this immense loss.
Today in our tears we honor this spirited Care Giver.

WILLIAMSON FAREWELL

This American Icon comes to our shores and steals our hearts.
The endless source of creative energy helped us along our way.
In addition to her teaching skills she still had time for ANS and ANB
Smoothing the machinery of our cultural and community goals,
She reminds us of long ago strength and beauty of our Founders.

We took a lesson in her sense of planning and determination.
We went along for the ride helping out in any way we could,
Our minds opened for possibilities taking on a newness.
Such a great teacher to come among us, greeting us in happiness.
I feel she has a special place in our blossoming lives.

A distant calling draws her away from this place.
Her life is taking on a new dimension of service.
Although we are saddened, our lives have been filled with praise.
The richness of her being with us will always be here.
She will be spreading her positive ways elsewhere.

She was seen dancing on campus and playing her guitar.
Sharing her talents often and planning fun events.

Her life of self giving shining like a Sitka summer day.
Our choir practiced on Thursdays and performed on Sundays.
Her voice with the others echoed throughout the church.

ANB gathers in appreciation with ANS for this Williamson farewell.
Duna made her mark in our hearts and minds by being here.
We rise triumphantly together to wish her the best life.
She has given us so much of herself, leaving us so improved.
Hats off to our living legend Duna Williamson.

THEY ARE IN OUR MEMORY

We gather in grief for those loved ones departed.
The oratory and music of our lives sing a sad song.
This ceremonial moment mirrors our tradition.
The caring and compassion we share this day.
Our hearts heavy for the lives lost last year.

We remember the beauty of their living lives.
They walked with us in the shining sunshine.
Like salmon making their last swim upstream
Their lives so full of purpose and worth.
We gathered around them in their closing moments.

In our memorial today we light the candles of hope.
Their names called out with deep sincerity.
We are surrounded with the light of life.
With some of us hearing the loss for the first time.
Our Tribal extensions are wide and we are tearful.

This is when our strength to carry on is needed.
We embrace one another and hold each closely.

Our clans unite in compassion for the families.
Understanding the needs of those grieving,
We will lift our lives with our own strength.

GEORGE MAX

The beloved family member George is gone.
I remember him as a child, youth, then man.
His life was caring for others with compassion.
It was how he lived that is so important.

In his earliest days I remember his joy of living.
I found his age eleven bicycle picture today.
Racing down Katlian Street in his red hat.
My most impressive telephoto photograph is
George and Richard Jacobs on Cottage rocks.

Mount Lake Terrace was my motorcycle visit.
The home of Harriet and Rosco Sr. in winter.
In summer they went North for fishing work.
Grandson George was there living with them.
The house was beautiful and far inland.

He also must have enjoyed Pelican summers.
We would occasionally enjoy his visits here.
We fished for trout and coho on the shore.

Bobby and Dickie would join us sometimes.
Charlotte would call for them at sunset.

Our coffee house visits were always a time of great joy.
A happy smile that knew no end, we talked at length.
A godfather to our daughter Sara Joy in her teens.
George and Diane did the work as Tribal Aunt and Uncle.
They brought the thing called "family" closer yet.

Captain of the "Diane" was a real Sitka outdoor adventure.
He ran the boat deep into the bays his ancestors knew well.

Many friends from all walks of life were his guests aboard that ship.
We sighted in his guns at the rifle range before hunting.
He wanted to be the best he could be out on the hunt.

It was his sunshine days we remember best.
His desire to improve the life of disabled people is well known.
Recognized by the State of Alaska for his efforts was rewarding.
Our entire family stood up in abiding praise for George.
We feel wealthy indeed for his walk through life with us.

ESTHER ANDERSON

A young man came to our Center calling on the Divine last week
And took we the grieving along with him in a sincere prayer.
We were surprised and also pleased at this act of courage.
His mother, Esther, our noon meal cherished friend
He recalled in loving memory for us all.

Cottage People know her well over the passing decades.
The Andersons lived two houses away from my family.
We harvested what the seasons gave us each year.
Often, we shared the wealth of the land and sea.
Deer, seal, ducks, geese, berries and clam.

Jenny and Lars knocked on our front door.
Jenny gave Elsie soap berries from Haines.
Their daughters Hazel and Esther giggled with
Jean and Charlotte out on the porch.
Together they cared about the details of
Human life always speaking of life beyond
The moment in their young lives.

Our church on the Crescent was a big part of our lives.
Our families often walked together from the Cottages.
Thanksgiving, Christmas, and Easter were special times.
My mind hears the Sheldon Jackson School choir sing the Messiah confidently.
After the services we would go to the Newell house for dessert.

Lars, Jenny, George, Lawrence, Esther, Hazel, and Helen
Were the Anderson family living on Kelly street.
Larry (FB) and George were our hunting partners often.
The Anderson ladies had lives of their own.

Berry picking, sewing and visiting with their SJS friends.

During World War II we had blackout practice.
Our windows were securely covered so no light came through.
On the attack alarms our families took to the woods.
The Andersons and Strands took cover in the same place.
No attack ever took place fortunately.

Esther was a lady special to my daughter Sara Joy.
She sends words of comfort to the Andersons today.
The message comes from Ada, Oklahoma their home.
Esther was the Christmas guest of Sara and Bill Brooks.

In her quiet way Esther always made friends easily.

At times I would talk with Esther at our noon lunches.
We would bring up the names of Lars and Jenny.
She would mention my parents Lila and John.
I had the feeling we were guardians of memory.
It was a refreshing journey into our past.

Gatherings like this bring us closer to our ancestors
And Tribal extensions who we need to cherish.
Esther shall ever be remembered kindly.
The beauty of her life is in our hearts.
Let's remember all the good she gave us.

Martin R. Strand Sr.

STREET WARRIOR REMEMBERED

July 10, 2003
Taking a hard look at grieving we came to Seattle.
Nephew, "TJ" is remembered in his own specialness.
After leaving Sitka his roots were firmly planted here.
As an uncle I often wondered how his life was going.
This recalls a sadness to my life about him.

Our Kaagwaantaan roots come from Eagle Nest House in Sitka.
His mother Sofia, also shares in this rich heritage.
We carry grandma, Elsie Newell Young's side of the clan.
Early on we floated positive images "TJ's" way.
The hope of a successful life was always on our minds.

We stood over his lifeless form.
His soul had long ago flown away on the 4th of July.
But the music of his life plays on over and over in our minds.
Our ocean of tears has to have some meaning.
Supporting each other we gained strength.

A community of cultural minds joined us spreading hope.
Our machinery had fought racial troubles the Elders suffered.

Grandpa "Koohúk" John Newell, from Snail House helped our advance.
No stranger to trouble Grandma Elsie forged ahead.
Our church and Elders found a path to the future.

This Kaagwaantaan "Street Warrior" also made his mark.
There was a beauty in his life that many people realized.
Fighting his fate as best he could was seen as a good sign.
His close friends rallied support from the sidelines.
Always his loving mother pointed a forward path.

Guilt of his uncle Martin, grew wanting to help in some way.
Looking for precious time but heavily involved in his family
And wanting to support the boys after the death of their father.
Months turned into years then decades rolled by till now.
Uncle Martin grieved his lack of resources to teach nephews.

I wished I could have remembered the mission statement of grandparents.
Something that could help me fashion a plan that would help.

ODE TO EFFIE HOOK

Marcia relates that Effie and her husband, Fritz witnesses the Justice of the Peace wedding of Arlene and Marcus just across the border at Galena, Illinois. Aunt Effie was Marcus's sister and was close to the Meyer family throughout her life. She willingly prepared 9 o'clock coffee and 3 o'clock tea and lived a good neighborly farm life that was both frugal and sensible. She loved to go to church activities of all kinds with her family. As a part of every meal a prayer must be said. She had a wonderful German inheritance and understood German when it was spoken. She was an often visitor on Sunday afternoons with grandma Gepka. She was the living legacy of Colfax Presbyterian Church. Even tempered and a good cook she was devoted to her children and was an expert on the sewing machine. This is dated December 7, 2005

We the Strands united in grief at the passing of Auntie Effie.
Heavy with remembrance for her steadfast life with us.
We like Darrell's writing wished our children had known her better.
She is an Iowan role model of strength and beauty.
The depth of her experience is a shining beacon to us all.

We walked through the Colfax cemetery on a sunny day.
Eldon was our guide and historian near the church.
The church, an integral part of her life I felt the warmth.
A true farm woman kept the workers well fed.
Set times of the day for rest and refreshment.

Into her 80's she had compassion for the elderly visiting
Them at their assisted living quarters bringing treats.
Living her life without complaint she always smelled the roses.
Her survival garden brought fruit with her tender care.
Always fresh bread on the table at the meals.

She was the moving, caring force for her church.

Intimately involved in its evolution from the beginning.
Taking such an active part in the mission outreach.
We see the results of her years of service to that goal.
We swell with pride at her life of accomplishment.

"For He who guides through the boundless sky thy certain flight
In the long way we must tread alone,
Will lead our steps aright."

RUTH DEMMERT

This poem written by Ruth Demmert of Kake was presented. It was written on April 28, 2005. Martin wanted it included. It was done in English and Tlingit. (Ed.)

Translation to :
"Dikee Aankaawu xat woo.eex"
Do not grieve for me.
I'm walking the path that God prepared for me.
I took His hand when He called me. I turned from life.

I could not add another day to laugh with you, to be with you.
I did not finish my work,
But at the end of that day, I had peace.

When you are lonely and sad for me, remember me with gladness.
We laughed together, we were friends. I too will miss this.

Don't despair because of sadness. The day will come again.
You will begin to see the sunshine, this is my hope for you.
My life was good with you, we had happy times.

Maybe I never fulfilled my life. Let me go without regret,
But look up towards heaven and in your heart you will know God had called me.

CHAPTER 3 THE GREATEST NATION IS SELF EXAMI-NATION

EIGHTEEN GOING ON THIRTY

It is the sparkle of her eyes I catch first.
It is her caring words as she talks of others.
She pours her whole life into a few sentences.
After reading those words it becomes clear
How important having a good life is to her.

A time of opportunity and also danger lurks.
Making good choices is all the more important.
Her bright view of her future life she reveals.
Wanting a fair chance comes out.
This is all that most of us ever wanted.

To let go and give her a chance.
To make sure she clears the manifold safely.
To hope her life turns out better than our own.
Her mind is music continuing to grow.
She looks for the good in everyone fearlessly.

I could speak of horrible pitfalls.
I could throw up caution flags.

I could live in continual worry.
But this is not my life to live.
Her destiny lies on a whole new plane.

It is more, "how can I help?"
It is opening challenging doors to the future.
It is presenting to her positive people.
In finding her dreams she calls on vision.
I must trust her life to be good.

Please call on your cultural ways.
Keep breaking new ground as a young woman.
Live our life without apology.
Do what is right to our way of thinking.
Care deeply for those closest to you.

AREAS LONG GONE

Looking at my life tonight I see needful areas long gone.
My musical listening is suffering greatly.
I whistle fewer songs from the many I have known.
Perhaps 8 to 10 songs are my current repertoire.

My upper whistle range is compromised by my hearing.
A lifetime of listening to great music is fading.
It was such a joy in the 90s to listen alone.
To let music speak to me in magical ways.

To mold my thoughts in artistic, creative times.
Now as my mind diminishes in capacity I falter.
It takes longer to identify familiar pieces I have known.
The Sitka Community Band is a help to my music.

I have opened doors to the past with this music.
The technique brings back old musical thoughts.
This could be the key to my late life growth.
To keep alert and active is my goal.

My Casio 670 keyboard brings me new happiness.
Voices I missed with my other keyboard are now there.
All I need to get started with my music software is a monitor.
256 color monitor will be my next improvement.

I've missed two Dog Point Fish Camp outings this year.
June and July are gone and I have August 18 to begin.
Part of me died just missing those important outings.

I will put my whole self into making the best of it.
There is so much I want to share of my life with others.

Martin R. Strand Sr.

ATTIC TREASURES

April 17, 1986 in the attic of 407 Sawmill on a rainy day at noon

The Southeast Music Festival is in town today. I got to wondering about when I was a youth in Sitka High so I went to the attic and opened that suitcase of memories. Right there where I left it was the 1952 Ketchikan Music Festival Program showing all the solos and ensembles and band pieces.

I found one of my First Rating solo sheets. The Sousaphone never did so well! It was already opened because there was no lock on it. It just revealed my Sitka family past in a single glance. There was my application for my first job at Mt. Edgecumbe. Letters from friends in High School around Southeast. Pictures of myself as a teenager. Letters from Mom and Dad. My old Bible packing girl friends. The yearbooks and graduation literature from Sitka High and Sheldon Jackson Junior College.

I even found a Sunday School attendance certificate for 1946. In 1956 Dad wrote to the Union about some benefits he needed to keep his family going. It may have been after he was injured at the Blue Lake Dam Project. I found the beginning of my photography when the bill from Capitol Camera in Columbus, Ohio followed me back to Sitka. It was for 42 more dollars due on my first Pentax H2!

There were graduation cards from the families around town. Just the other day I did granddaughter pictures for Keith Snowden. In 1955 he handed me my diploma at Sitka High. Daisy and Pete Jones sent me a card.

Mary Prescott tutored me in public speaking. I found a monologue about, "Man and the Mosquito." Tonight (4/17/86) I went home and copied it on the computer. It's listed under The Islands in the Sky.

Today there were no tears, just joy at re-living those happy years. I know I am going to the attic again soon!

A VISIT TO GRANDPA NEWELL

October 6, 2000
This talk was given to a fifth grade class at the grave site of John Newell.
It's good to be with you today, grandfather, John Newell.
Elvia, who is learning and loves our culture asked me to come here.
Her class of bright eyes and minds are also gathered around this place.
When I was a young man I came here to learn poetry.
I would sit and read out loud words of famous poets.

It was a cold day in 1940 when we brought you out here.
I was only five years old and you were my first lost relative.
I would be making many trips here in the years to come.
Tuberculosis had taken many of our friends and relatives.
I had it at the age of three but I survived.

Your people from Snail House in Hoonah came for the 40 day party.
It was the final grieving and celebration of your life's achievements.
Koohúk is your Tlingit name but we called you Grandpa Eesh.
Your daughter, my mother Lila Newell Strand is at the City Cemetery.
Grandma Elsie is also there.

Grandma Elsie married your nephew, Ralph Young, my second grandfather.

When I was 8 and 9 he took me on the "Smiles" to Nakawisina.
We put up smoked dry fish for the winter at our camp.
The women would pick berries in the afternoon and I would scare away
The bears with a can with pebbles in it shaking it vigorously.

Here other close friends of yours are buried.

Before the cemetery it was our custom to cremate those who passed away.
We did not take up precious land as we do today.
At night animals walk through here or rest on their way to Indian River.
I hope your eternal rest is not interrupted by shooting at the Trooper Academy.

CHRISTMAS 2003

Swirling rapidly, this year is coming to an end. Days flashing by, by the square root allowed me to express myself. Where did it all go? Am I any better than I was in 2002? It is the time of year that I take stock of my life and its effect on others near to me.

In January, 2002, I wrote poetry for the Middle School's Martin Luther King Day. In February, I presented one of my works on Elizabeth Peratrovich, Tlingit civil rights activist who brought our cause forward. I was ten years old when Elizabeth and Roy Peratrovich visited us on their way to Juneau to speak to the legislature.

Proud to be a part of Sitka Community Band I played the tuba in our Spring concert April 8th. It is great being part of a musical team bringing joy to the town when we perform. In April this year I played "Asleep in the Deep" a theme and variations of an early solo I did in 1953.

We traveled to Sandy, Oregon in June to visit our son, Martin, Jr. and his family. Tyler and Shelby are his children and his wife is Cherie. While there my sister, Sofia, lost her son T J on the 4th of July. I did a eulogy in Seattle.

I was Vice President of Alaska Native Brotherhood this last year. It was quite a journey for me but I was up to it. I presented much of my written work for ANB and ANS from time to time.

CLOSING OF ANOTHER YEAR

December 31, 1997

What will the future bring in my life! How much more time do I have? How will old age have an effect on my living and when does it begin?

Most of the year has been free from pain and suffering that I have known. I will not reflect on the closing days of 1995 which was a wake-up call for me. People who have had Angioplasty, rumor has it that they have complications within three years after the procedure. What does this mean? I have been listening and reading all I can about heart disease. If I am careful about my diet, exercise and cholesterol level, I might not have any complications down the road. I have ridden my bikes with confidence all year but have ice and snow on the ground right now. I hope it is brief so I can ride daily.

Exactly how is my health today? Last week I had trouble with a cold that brought sore muscles to my central chest. Why does it have to be so near my heart! I called the helpful nurse at 966-2411 and explained the situation and took a Tylenol. That did well for me for two days. Today my foot was sore and I limped somewhat. I don't know what brought that on. I'm taking baby aspirin (81mg) each day and then for the evening meal I take Lovastatin (20 mg) for cholesterol control. Martina is sending me 60 tablets of it from Anchorage which I get from Alaska Regional.

Last November and this December I have had a spurt of activity for the outdoors. For $100.00 I bought a reloading RCBS Rock Chucker press and it came with hundreds of dollars of accessories. I loaded 223 caliber ammo along with 30-06 ammo. Of course, I tested it at the range with several successful visits. My powder and bullet supply went rapidly and today I put together a list of reloading dies (I have some extra) and bullets that I will be trading with other shooters. My groups at the Range have been about 11 ½" at 100 yards. That is pleasing, but with practice I can do better. When I go to the Range I take a stool and sandbags and targets that I make myself on the computer. I use round red labels to cover the bullet holes so I save on targets. The bullets and powder are expensive downtown. I have a reloading catalog coming from Midway supply soon.

I'm only a shadow of my former self when it comes to photography. I have no darkroom to process negatives or prints. Perhaps I can work something out in 1998? I miss printing and processing negatives. I have a goodly supply of chemicals and my photographic paper has all but died being stored in the bathroom near a hot radiator. I thought of using Sheldon Jackson's darkroom or the UAS darkroom but I don't know what strings would be attached. I wondered if Shee Atika or Sitka Tribes of Alaska would have space for me to work. I will look into this next month (January). I have some good working equipment for processing or picture taking. With my computer I'd like to make an inventory for myself and others so I can sell or trade some of it for film and paper. For years I've gone out of town and picked up slightly outdated film and paper. That is how I have run my business.

DESTINY

January 2, 1986

With each passing day I see with greater clarity the destiny my life will fulfill. I have lived quite a full life in a wide spectrum of joy and sorrow. I am beginning to see why I did things. There seems to be a pattern of activities in my lifestyle.

Am I going to play the deck that fate dealt me? Is there another purpose to my life I know little about? Am I approaching the end of my life soon?

I could cry about my summer illness and its after-affects. I think there was a reason I was given this illness to see my own mortality. Like Scrooge in "The Christmas Carol" I was given a glimpse of myself, past, present, and future.

It is not a beautiful sight. I have not been the ideal, caring, compassionate human being I should have been. I get my clues from my life as a father, uncle, Tribal being. I just seem to not have time to work at these roles. Maybe I just don't care anymore. Maybe I feel I've lived as full as I am going to live. Perhaps the challenges of life are not as real to me as they should be.

1986. What a year? I poked along with minimum output and then got sick. My cries of real pain in the hospital let me know that I wanted to live. I'm glad that I followed through with my Kake School pictures. This was a real attempt to show that I could be worthwhile to myself and family. I needed very much to follow through with this project. I waited twelve days before I sent out the order. Some of those days were necessary to rationalize the order sequence. But I did it! 1986 triumph! Kake liked my work and perhaps I will do it again.

It's good to treat the customer as if they mattered in your life. I hope I can have this spirit always.

DREAMS OF MARTIN STRAND

June 3, 2004

The dawning of a new day, a day of opportunity?
Beethoven playing wildly, Concerto #3 making its way around the room.
I cried the other day just listening to it and what my life might have been.
The intense beauty of the music crafted with such glorious rhythms.
An ancient longing in my heart swells up strong.

69 years blown away so rapidly leaving me breathless!
Wondering what life was about and my part in it.
Looking forward with expectation about the final outcome.
How rich and full was my life in the many passing seasons?
Where is it all leading and has it been very meaningful?

I am in the last movement of this Concerto called life.
It is not a sad time and not without some happiness.
The music of it all dwells and lingers in my memory.
The important things have been done so far.
Worthy meaning is all part of the big picture.

Birds flying by my window purposeful with intent.

Rushing to their season to prepare their young for flight.
Every moment of their lives is important to their goal.
Their young so dependent and waiting for the meal.
Growing strength of their wings is coming to them.

My flight to the future is slow and measured.
Taking up the loose ends and tying the knots tightly.
What kind of planning should I be doing?

The music gives me ideas on how my life should go.
Its message presents the highest ideals of a good life.

The sea calls me to come out and play.
The mountains beckon towards their mystery.
The sun creeps into my room telling me time is flying.
The red-breasted sap sucker taps a rhythm on a telephone pole,
I must get out and enjoy this glorious day.

Martin R. Strand Sr.

FILLING MY LIFE WITH HAPPINESS

My health is very good at this time. It's been three months since I had trouble with my heart. The angioplasty was a complete success. I was in Anchorage only for a short time. Martin, Jr. came up to be with me during my procedure. I was glad he came. Now I'm back to 100%.

Last night I paid my dues for ANB; then I read a poem highlighting early ANB men I had known at the hall. The crowd loved it and applauded my work. I plan to do more poems in the upcoming meetings.

Jimmy Davis is in town briefly. He and I used to hang out and play pool from time to time in the past. He left a pool cue with me before he left town the last time.

From Midway, USA, I ordered a BSA Red Dot Sight for my 223 Interarms Mark II rifle. I plan to use it for sea otter, seal and deer. I can quickly change scopes for different conditions. The new sight can be used on rifles or pistols and this will make my battle station operational.

ANB Grand Camp convention will be in Ketchikan for a week in November. I hope to be a delegate from our local group. We have three to four delegates go to convention each year.

That's the news about my life so far and I'll keep you informed about any changes.

There were 50 coho in a school in Indian River today. The tide was coming in and the wind was picking up rapidly when I first spotted the fish. Excitedly I biked home to get my gear ready for fishing. I decided to use my bait casting rod and reel. It's the one that I bought last year to fish for king salmon at Sawmill Creek. At that time I caught my first river king. Today I made only a few casts and ZINGO I had a 10 pound coho in Jamestown Bay. I made a cast ahead of the school and one came after and struck. I had to cut my fishing short when Ralph Guthrie paged me three times about my new board position on Alaska Studies for our school system. I hope I can contribute well to the group.

The good news about my computer is I now have Windows 98 CD Rom software. Last month I installed a Seagate 2.1 Gigabyte hard drive. I needed Windows 98 to configure my printers. It cost $179.00 and I paid $75.00 down. The bad news is I found bugs in my Lotus Smart Suite software. Disk #17 has a problem.

The Teen Center wants me to set up a pool tournament for the teens this fall. They also want me to put up a gallery of my pictures for their Coffee Shop opening this Friday (October 1st). In addition they want me to do poetry readings.

DOWN BUT NOT OUT

December 1, 2006

Today lifeless staring out my window looking deeply.
Hope, only a distant memory, fades into the grayness.
Wondering what the future holds heavy on my mind.
Uncertainty of the times where the wind blows.
Life less than it used to be sings an ever sad song.

The cold of ice under my feet reaches deep into my heart.
The pulse slows under the pressure of living.
Ever reaching into the underlying plot I seek help.
Changes unknown to me now deepen the mystery.
The low resources is such a reality I want to forget.

Buoyed by music full of purpose, a fainting glimmer of hope.
Perhaps, Shostakovich would speak to me now.
His music weaves a strange tale of mostly sadness.
A real reflection of my state of mind looking ahead.
A sudden chill runs through my body at the thought.

What kind of contribution can I make for the betterment?
Can I give the world something better for my being here?

Not doing anything creative in such a long time grieves me.
Work undone piles heavy on my mind and oh, the guilt!
Waiting for something good to happen that never happens.

AMERICAN ST

FEBRUARY 20, 2008

It is my wish to be a more complete person in every way. There is a loneliness in my life that is taken care of by my music. It is my emotional heart beat that suggests a rhythm I can easily follow toward my goals. It lifts my soul yearning to newer more powerful heights. What am I without music?

The ability to create is a good part of my life. My new digital camera will fulfill my creative leanings to a great extent. I am learning the joys and limitations of this new, exciting medium. I am ready to explore multiple exposures and the editing process that the software provides. I am only limited by my own small visions. The possibility of growth is immense. I am working out the details and procedures to get to my dreams end.

The ability to see something artistically is still with me from early times. I must reach out and avoid the clichés that have plagued my thoughts of the past. Having a fresh look at old images in new light is what I am all about. To be original takes a lot of imagination that I desperately need. I now have the tools to go forward with new strength and imagination. The only thing that would distract me would be my loss of focus. I must look forward and not back in my images and my writing.

Gathering my written works is my project at hand right now. I want very much to catalog the work for easier editing. This is so important for myself and my editor. In the back of my mind are the images I want to enhance the book of my work. An outline of the chapters should be one of the first components to come about. When that is done I want to add the narration before each poem for the reader to understand more fully. The work will go to the editor to review and come back to me for further comments or corrections. Where the pictures will be placed will be the next step in the long procedures. Then the chapters will come into being along with any footnotes and additional input. The pacing of the poems is important at this time. I would hope they will be in proper contrast and cohesive in thought. The final format changes will be in order long before the publishing. I want to make the writing user friendly for the editor and the reader.

I will be open to creative suggestions at all times. I will discuss the details in a civil manner and try to give my best shot at explaining my rationale. I will put forward a positive attitude wanting to complete the book. I have lots to learn from the experience and will focus toward that end. This is a journey I will complete.

There should be a time set to accomplish the work. I am considering an early morning starting time and sticking to it. There also should be an evening time to review what I have done. Proof reading is a must and the corrections be made as soon as possible. I am hoping to minimize distractions each and every time I begin my work. It is also a chance to explore my true feelings about the project. As time and energy permit I will work toward this gift that has been handed to me. I must complete the work in a timely manner, hoping I am not too late in finishing my book. My meditation is in motion and will continue to be bringing my thoughts forward.

It is the beginning of a book of poetry by myself. My wandering mind looks for clues as to what I have done that is important and appealing to the universal audience. Most of what I've written is about people of Sitka and our region. Since I am a memorial poet my writing deals with details I remember about their lives as they affected me.

Each summer I join the Dog Pont Fish camp in June, July, and August. We teach children 7 to 15 about our culture and how to live off the land. We sharpen our hunting and fishing skills and food gathering. I have written on location essays about our activities and why we do them. I reflect an ancient echo my grandparents taught me about living in fish camp. My writing is about those days of my 8th and 9th years with grandparents on the boat "Smiles." There is a deep longing in my writing for the lessons of those days long ago. I live for camp life as we prepare for Fall and Winter.

About my photography. I am something of a Sitkan historian when it comes to pictures. While I was at Ohio State University I began taking pictures in the late 1950's. I bought a Practica F3 camera with a normal lens and 180mm Telemongor 5.6. I cruised the Olentangy River and photographed turtles, carp, and Black fishermen. While bus riding, the camera helped me express myself with people pictures. I soon noticed a Pentax H1 camera at the High Street Camera shop and put $10.00 down and $10.00 per month and it was mine. The Practica camera used the same lenses and so it was a wise purchase. Hanging out at the Fine Arts department I photographed campus life. I moved into the George Wells Knight International House on campus. It was an eye opener for this Sitka boy. Surrounded by foreign nationalists intent on following the American dream rubbed off on me.

Soon I was on the campus radio station, WOIO, pursuing radio speech/education. My experience at Sitka's KSEW put me ahead of my peers in the communications aspects of radio. Some of the poetry I'd learned in Sitka came in handy for English Literature classes. I had some broadcast time at the station and did quite well. The radio department had a lot of interest for students at that time. It was competitive and that grabbed my interest. With the contacts I made my sponsor Fred Palmer soon got me a night job on WTVN. I had the 5 P.M. to 1 A.M. shift. It was something of a request program and I talked to people all night and played music of their choosing. In the summer time I worked for the Columbia Stove Company. We loaded stoves to export in boxcars.

In my senior year I was called home at the death of my father, John S. Strand. My mother Lila called and I returned home. At the airport, Austin van Pelt said, "You are going on the air tomorrow," and I did. I was on the air quite often and classified records for the record library. I did commercials for various businesses and had a Sunday afternoon music and poetry show. It gave me an opportunity to read many works of great poets throughout history. Several years later I joined KIFW commercial radio and TV. I worked there until 1977. I also used the studio to refine my photographic skill as a portrait photographer.

What has been exciting in my life that I want to share with others? What insights do I have that would be worthwhile to an audience? Can I give sufficient detail in what I describe to that audience? How good is my memory for details decades away? There seems to be whole blocks of memory missing in certain times of my life. Occasionally I visit my past in dreams full of the smallest details. Who will be my target audience? What will be my mission to reveal important events I have lived? Shall I focus on a narrow interesting part of my life experiences or reach out in broader context? Is my use of grammar up to par for this project? Am I big enough to take creative analysis of my work?

Martin R. Strand Sr.

GRASPING FOR A LITTLE TRUTH IN LIFE

September 7, 2001

Walking to town lazily thinking of what I am doing today.
Filling my lungs with air polluted with car exhaust fumes in the rain.
Diesel is blowing against me in a black cloud.
I used to breathe deep on my way to band practice.
It worked for me in lengthening my breath for tuba playing.

It's not what's wrong with the world today that bothers me.
It's the darkened atmosphere so deadly we live in around us.
Untrusting people with agendas not well thought out.
Singing their own song at the expense of others.
Not walking in the shoes that somehow don't fit.

Part of my life is the problem that others can see.
They are good at criticizing my every movement around town.
I don't hate them for that; it just makes me a little sad.
I'm spending my life in quality times that others don't understand.
Picking the battles I want to fight and discarding others.

It is such a living city that surrounds us and gives breathing room.

It forgives and cares about the paths we walk daily.
We drink of its beauty and rely on its wisdom.
It shares our dreams as we lovingly relate to each other.
It is more than luck that we are all drawn here.

I dream of hunting again but I have few places to put up my game.
I long for fishing king salmon in the opened streams.
My kayak lies dormant and often at night it calls for me.
So busy am I that I now only faintly pay attention to its cry.

I must commit myself to growing back to Nature.

My bike is so friendly to my body and my only exercise.
After riding, my mind runs free to think up new dreams.
A game of solitaire in the morning charts my day.
It seems like I'm doing nothing but I'm reading my fortune.
Refreshed in spirit I then go out into the world I love.

A season of friendly tourists greets my gaze at Victoria's.
I wonder at the stories of their lives away from home.
Connected by cell phones everywhere how can they enjoy the trip?
There is a sadness in seeing this connective spirit so wide spread.
But they do so much for our city, how could I complain?

Slighted again, I push forward not knowing what to expect.
Likening myself to others of the same persuasion I creep.
Billeted with delight, a sense of knowing overcomes me.
Blighted with success that is not deserved I wonder.
Lightning--like moving mind I come upon solutions.

Willingly shapes form all over me cutting off my blood.
Mysterious movements grasp longingly on my arm.
Serious times wrap themselves around my girth.
Letters fly in the wind and paste themselves on my head.
Messages from where I know not, speak directly to my soul.

INFINITY

October 24, 2000

Reaching deep into my soul I'm lost in its shallowness.
My sense of purpose is an illusion, rarified by time.
The spark of ambition lacks power to ignite my fire.
Shadows of things to come darken my thoughts.
I hasten to approach the great mystery before me.

Wanting so much more out of life than I'm given
I stand alone facing what might happen to me.
Action without my consent and not knowing when.
A sardonic smile moves slowly over my lips.
Humor in the face of danger seems the only answer.

It's not sadness that bothers me more than usual.
It's not marking of time that is slipping away.
It's the uncertainty of my footprints into the future.
Keyed into and locked into my fate with no changes possible.
The chains that bind me rattle in terror.

It's a sweet terror that stretches my life forward.

The fear is not great but quite forgiving.
Knowing that I've accomplished something with my life
Reduces that strangeness I've felt before.
My will to express hardens with time.

I view the brief life of the creatures full of meaning.
I see myself caught in the mix of living things.
My small voice cries universal mutterings so faintly.
My eyes see infinity light years ahead and beyond.
My thoughts are big and must be said with faith.

Spending my time meaningfully with the Seasons is all I ask.
My discontent is muted with the advent of reality.
Another day of opportunity wakens me from a dark night.
Relationships grow deeper as I move along.
My temporal blindness makes me feel the less I see.

LOOKING AROUND THE CORNER AM I

April 22, 2000

How many more mornings will I wake up to see the sun?
How many walks to town do I have left?
How many birds will I count during their migration?
How many kayak trips will I take to the open sea?
How many grandchildren will I hear their laughter?

The answer is "some more would be nice."
When will I next get sick and flirt with death?
How long will it be before I am doomed to a wheelchair?
How many more times will people be glad to see me?
Will I travel North or South sometime soon?

Who will take my music seriously and enjoy my CD collection?
My prints and negatives need to be taken care of before I go.
My will desperately needs to be done while I am still able.
My tape collection of events needs a new home.
What will become of my writing, who will want it?

I've been wanting to write this for so long.

It has been bubbling up to the top of my mind often.
Some kind of closure needs to be done about my life.
I've lived a rich, full life up to now and I need to share.
The things I've learned might be valuable to someone.

I am so cluttered and I don't think I can get out of it.
So much is left undone in so many areas.
If I could do just a little every day it would help.
I have to care more about the important things in my life.

The needed spark of inspiration is not there.

I'm reminded often of my wretchedness from waking to the remains of the day.
The key is in my mind and needs to be opened while I am able.
The most creative thing I do now is my writing.
It's the only thing I can do with some confidence.
I've been hoping it would move me to some kind of action.

HOT NEWS

August 30, 1986

I wondered why I had such difficulty throwing away or burning the Wall Street Journal. It has given me such a lift at every reading. It meant so much to my informational self that it seemed so wrong to burn or throw it away. I would have liked to share the excitement with others or at least my family.

It is already written and ready to be filed in which ever file I wanted. Then the thought occurred to me, 'we live in a constantly changing world.' Change is daily, hourly, minutely, secondly. Why save old news? Is there any value reading something so close to history? Maybe if it were five years old, ten or twenty years old it could be of some value. But last week's Wall Street Journal? Can you understand my dilemma?

We must move on no matter how painful. When we think we have valuable information we would pass on to others thus giving them another perspective of our times. So the paper serves another useful purpose. To start our fires.

I wish I were that useful. I wish I could contribute something meaningful, lasting and beautiful. Is there something in my life worth that much?

LIFE OF A PHOTOGRAPHER

December 9, 1985

The answering service has hit pay dirt. I heard from George who's in desperate state. His rent is due this Thursday and needs $450.00 by that time. I wish I could give it to him. But the best I could do is trade. He thinks his Mamiya 645 is worth over $1,000.00. I mentioned that there are repair charges for what I did for his lenses. Also work on the camera. In his state of mind he'll want to take the equipment and sell it. He'll find that he can get maybe $250.00 at best and possibly less. I think I will approach him on taking a lens for my rental and work.

The 45mm lens would be the best for my purposes. His view finder is not working properly and he doesn't want to hear about any troubles with his camera. I might suggest that he sell some of his Minolta equipment. He could possibly cover his rent with that system. I'm not going to shell out any money on this deal. Do I owe him anything? I think so. I have several negatives of his I haven't printed. So, I'm obligated to do something generous. But I repeat NO MONEY!

On other subjects: This Wednesday after High School gets out Missie will call. I have to do her portrait. Outdoors would be preferred. She paid in advance and has two 3x5 in folders paid. Expect a call about 3:30 p.m.

I have to pick up the Minolta of Bob who's now from Kake. He left his camera with Reggie Peterson on Oja Way across from the Taxidermy Shop. The camera was in a fire and scorched on the outside. I'm to cosmetically repair the outside and check the operation. Insurance is allegedly paying for the repair. Don't let it go without payment.

I have to break the news to Laurel about the bad negative I did for her. The light from the kitchen at 407 leaked onto the darkroom and fogged the complete edge of the film. I have some images that are affected only a little and others are no good. I'm giving them a new roll of film and free processing as a concession for the loss. I hope that's enough.

LOOKING AT MY LIFE FROM A DISTANCE

September 10, 2003

Dreams of my future life and work clutter my thoughts tonight. There is so much to be done and so little time for those dreams to come to reality. I am in a deep state of meditation constantly looking for an answer that will address my problems.

What would I want to do with the rest of my life? I think it has to start with my cleaning up my house, 10% of which is valuable. Things I have not touched for over 10 years and beyond must be considered for release.

Dreams of a darkroom and superior sound system are drifting far away from me. Video editing, photographing flying dragon flies, kayak trips around Sitka, hunting deer, and keyboard composing will have to wait their turn in the priorities that God has given me.

I'm gathering in my mind the importance of ANB Grand Camp in Ketchikan at the end of this month. I must do something important there to bring honor to my local camp and myself. I should write about my Tribal family and their place in Indian politics. The love and care they gave to their mission as great human beings. Their dedication to being excellent in everything they did. I am part of that history and must take my place there. My laptop should be in good condition for the trip and I need a good, small printer. I may be called upon to do some scribe work while there. The memorial service program is one of my priorities and should be. My Tribal extensions should be made plain and honor given to them wherever I can.

The poetry I've done is worthy of reading while at Grand Camp somewhere in the program. I should let them know I have it ready. I take my work with me wherever I go but never let them know I have it ready in time. I want to memorialize Richard Carle, my school mate from the 1950's who learned poetry like myself. I will read his favorite impressive poem. The Monday after Grand Camp we have convention reports and I plan to have the most complete, detailed report I have ever done!

This letter to myself is long overdue. I want to analyze my life often about at least once a year to see how I'm doing in the community. I am involved on several fronts that I enjoy. Sitka Community Band is on Tuesdays again. So is the Greater Sitka Pool League. We have a new league president, Woody Widmark, who might make some significant changes for the better unless negative forces grab hold of him early on. Perhaps, league could meet on Wednesday or Thursday evenings? SJC meets for teleconference this Monday afternoon. We have some important issues to discuss. President Haaland sees a conflict of interest in a board member being on campus on the board. I disagree strongly! Alumni are Alumni and should be welcomed constantly.

Soon the bird migration will be flying in Sitka Sound. I hope I can be there when they do and enjoy their traveling lives. I want Gary to see them as I did when I was his age. There are fewer now but still there. I have all the equipment necessary to photograph them when they get here. I think I need some of those new bird books about Alaska.

Video editing is on my mind. I want to install my CD burner to my computer and use the Fire Wire to connect to the video camera. I hope to have a sound card with left and right sound slots for the best quality. I am looking at Dan E's video editing program and I think I can do the editing software. I have to install my 30 gigabyte hard drive as a slave to my 4.4 gigabyte hard drive for the editing programs. I will also use the computer system to record audio material I recorded decades ago for family history. I have to install a high density card in the computer slot with the special card. My editing battle station will then be complete.

My Dog Point experience earlier this month was outstanding even though we had fewer students. I loaded 223 rifle ammunition and critically sighted in my Mauser 223 at 65 yards. We had a chance to get to know the staff and we talked of our goals for the camp and were fed very well the entire time. I wrote five pages of poetry there from my typewriter I left at the camp. We saw two deer and I shot at two seal but they got away from our bouncing boat. We were rain soaked on the hunt and welcomed the warm Dog Point Hilton that day. I found my survival kit matches were defective. I'm glad I was not out in the woods. The matches burned out when scratched against a rock. They don't make matches like they used to.

Friday I played organ, piano and synthesizer at the Lutheran Church for some tourists. They enjoyed it and I needed the practice. I feel it's my Norwegian connection in Sitka and usually play several times during the tourist season.

Sheldon Jackson College is going and I've been playing pool with the students. I've been raising the level of their skills at the table. We play 8 ball, 9 ball, 7 ball, and Line Pool. I try to show them the options during the game and one of those options is to miss to put our opponent in a bad position. This is hard for some of them to understand since most of them play what I call "Code of the West." I teach them to "take care of yourselves" in a competitive way. Some of them are beginning to show talent and skill.

There is so much more I want to say about my life and its problems. Writing like this has been part of my life since the 1970's and beyond. It is sort of therapy to see where I'm going and how I relate to others. I read past papers I've done and notice some of the same problems come up as history has a way of repeating itself.

Martin R. Strand Sr.

MARTIN STRAND ON A COLD NIGHT

October 20, 2001

It is such a joy to know that I have a good skill level.
Advancing in music is so much better for me now.
I am remembering my early musical days in high school.
Some of the music we play brings back sweet memories.

There is so much I want to do in video production.
The excellent GL1 video camera can scratch that itch.
Recorded music with sensitive narration I can do easily.
I need editing equipment badly to do the job right.
I will be ready with new poetic ways to speak.

My writing needs to increase if I get to go to Convention.
I must take my work and find an audience for it.
My outlook on Tlingit culture in Sitka needs expression.
I need to do an original piece for a memorial service.
I might read the one I did for last year's service.

The laptop computer will go with me to Kake.
I'm setting up and testing the Epson Action writer printer.

I have two printer ribbons which should be enough.
It would be good to learn more about Resolution making.
I need the convention format to do that.

What are my chances of being elected as a delegate?
I have been visible for the past two years at ANB.
I read my reports of significant events over those years.
It's good to have something ready to say at these events.
I hope this is remembered when voting time comes.

I'm Vice President of Tlingit and Haida Sitka Chapter this year.
We meet Sunday the 21st at 1 P.M. at the ANB hall.
If Mark is not there I will be in charge of the meeting.
We have a rough agenda I think I can handle.
I hope we have a good turnout this time.

My 300 Winchester Magnum is a Mauser Interarms gun.
It is my hope to load 165 grain Silver/Lead bullets for it.
The powder I use will be 4064 Imperial at 45 grains.
All I have to do is install copper gas checks.
It is a reduced load good for seal, sea otter, and deer.

Listening to my mind racing through its paces I lament.
The music of my memories grasps a theme foreboding.
The forward thrust of my life stagnates, slowly.
Wanting to do so much for myself and others is in the shadows.
Wondering where all this will lead is wrapped in mystery.

The feeling of accomplishment evades my today thinking.
Moving around to position myself positively is not there.
My record of things done is sometimes impressive.
Willingness to expand my horizon is always nearby.
Can my mind be so open to grasp new thoughts?

Relating to my new band brightens my mind.
The possibilities of creating something beautiful is now.
Piano, electronic keyboard, or tuba visit my thoughts.
The longing to do music has always been with me.
There is no question that I have the time to do this now.

My kayak is on the back burner for the present.
I wish I could carry hunting equipment and deer.
It is so small for this kind of action.

Lamenting the loss of my big kayak lives with me still.

This is the reason for my so few trips this year.

I'm growing towards being computer literate.
My music and midi keyboard programs have flaws.
That something is wrong with the CD system plagues me.
I want to be fiercely independent of others.
Asking for help sometimes is difficult for me to do.

I have thoughts of starting to print pictures again.
There is no reason for me to hold back the work.
I do not have a darkroom at home so I must go elsewhere.
I often wonder what obligations to others I would have.
If I could print pictures for others undisturbed.

This year I will have to give up billiards league again.

MY END OF THE YEAR FEARLESS INVENTORY 2005

This turned into a tradition.
Alone at my writing my mind reaches ahead.
Still seeking to be relevant in any way I can.
Living the life as an artist pent up in uptightness.
Legacy is on my mind and how important is it?
Have I given back enough to the life I have lived?

The emptiness of a distant family is heavily with me.
The time I should be sharing is taken away.
Listening to my serious music in melancholy of the moment
I hear the sadness of a minor key tugging at my heartstrings.
Who is left for me to give what I have.

What time I have left I should be constantly writing.
There is this urge to say something worthwhile.
I miss using words and music together to express myself.
They mean so much more when used together.
It is a reflection of a time I made a better contribution.

There will be a time when I cannot create and that frightens me.

A time when I will not care to be active as I have been.
I wonder how it will be when my mind slowly fails?
I see so many of my peers not making a contribution.
Perhaps, just to show up for another day.

Right now I am pushing my talents to the forefront.
Knowing that I have to use and express them while I can.
I took an inventory of all the poetry I have committed to memory.
The list is growing smaller as each decade passes.
I find I must listen to deeper music before I forget it.

In the past I would whistle long passages of concert music.
I would sing in joy and sadness melodies remembered.
I miss my concert programs that enriched my living.
I want to memorize poetic works, including my own.
Perhaps, I should record what I have written?

It is the end of the year 2005, my 70th year.
As is my custom I will write a fearless inventory of my life this year.
It is not without happiness and I have done many good things.
I feel the need to tell the story of my family while I can.
Perhaps, this small laptop can contain in total my life story.

MUSIC TELLS ME

Silently the night looms into darkness.
The light of day slowly fades over many hours.
Whitened clouds turn shades of gray and dark gray.
The seagulls make their move to some distant shore for the night.
The evening trill of robins displays chromatic music in tranquility.

Setting my chart way out there past the colorful horizon
Where the petrel flies on a stormy sea.
Floating mind upsets my balance as if teetering from a tree.
What will the future hold and when will it end?
Rising tide dashes against the shore with renewed confidence.
The wind lifting the salt sea spray to the plants above.

Waiting trout surface for the flies inches above the water.
Up to my neck in the cold water numbing my feet and arms.
I slowly make my way to the welcome shore exhausted.
Strength comes back to my limbs in the warm night air.
Birds of the night circle in mystery flight above me.
Sitting on the weathered log I recount the day's events.

Searching for a meaningful life seems more distant than before.
Lost track of the trail means I have to wait for light.
The woods silently sing a song of the night around me.
Imagined danger is most feared if only in the mind.
Dancing lights of boats passing way out there in the sound.
Alone on the darkened shore the hours start adding up.

The chill reaches deep although summer warmth is in the air.
Why should I long to come home on a night like this?
Change runs deep as a bottomless sea with tortured waves above.
Overcome with emotional shivering as a light wind comes up.

I must start a fire soon before it is too late.
Pitch laden young spruce brush is nearby and lights to a match.

Head pain with each passing step increases where no medicine can cure.
Steps unsure, stumble on the rocks below, I catch myself from falling.
Future flies before me at a quickened speed I cannot understand.
I reach out to find my way blinded by my own doing.
Calling to the ancients to lift me away from the gathering danger.
Music tells me all about my life up to now and where it is going.

MY REFLECTION

The bucket of tears is overflowing with new purpose.
A strange emptiness erupts carrying me with it.
Reaching into my past comes to haunt me.
Living over and over again my mistakes.
An overpowering light flashes a new kind of pain.

Terrible truth: that a heart awakened to a great love
Is also opened to great pain.
Family fleeing away at light-year speed surrounds me.
The likelihood of coming back is so remote.
My life hanging in the balance by a thread.

Prokofiev's Symphony #1 plays my feelings today.
Confused, depressed, is the musical treatment.
The building emotion of a people reflects sadness.
It is not without resolution or hope.
Movement toward solution it strongly suggests.

Some day, perhaps soon, communication will open.
Being the subject of such hatred is difficult.

How can the blame be equally spread?
Do I have ownership of the blame?
Is there anything in my life worthwhile?

Prokofiev suggests dialog in a constant stream.
He also suggests searching for answers.
It is such a dark side of life I see before me.
Perhaps, there is a path back to reality?
Listening suggests hard work ahead of me.

I get up in the morning and go about my business.

My bike defines my motor skills for another day.
Numeric meditation (cards) moves my mind.
I can relate to numbers as a problem solver.
Thank goodness I still have some friends.

MY LIFE TODAY

July 21, 2002

A deep loneliness shifts into my life at this time in my thinking. Where am I going and is there forward movement away from the sadness that hovers over me in oppression. The reasons for my being trapped in a vicious circle of doom has many tentacles covering what I do. Life blood ebbing away in my troubled mind seems to end.

It all gathers around my not having the adequate resources needed to live a quality life. Lack of planning for my retirement shows up often as I think about it. Most likely, I will not travel on my own to Anchorage in August as I planned. Whenever I bring up my wishes to travel I am shot down by negative expressions as if I won't visit my family there. I never get to tell the truth of why I want to travel alone to look for camera equipment and computer supplies.

I wish I could go up there early or stay late but that is not to be. Others have me programmed for only a brief stay after I have some kidney tests that SEARHC wants me to have. It is true I want to see friends in addition to my family up there. I could do a lot of good for myself and family. I know I could. There is such a distorted view of my life that I cannot explain to others without confronting negative thoughts on their part. As a result of these expressed negative thoughts I will be stressed in body and spirit and this could affect my much-needed tests.

I don't really ask for much in my living lifestyle. Perhaps, I am too selfish with the way I live. I have a small group of friends that care about me in special ways. They appreciate my poetry and musical talents and excellent conversation each day. However, there are those that believe that I am too free with my life and they feel threatened that I succeed. There are those that are outwardly friendly but I could not trust them and therefore I share very little of my life with them. Some of them share everything going on in their lives with no editing out of their troubles. It is as if they are reaching out in desperation looking for some kind of help. I hope I have never given out that kind of impression. Maybe, they think I am strong because I don't spill out my life's grief and woes.

My Tribal life has had its ups and downs over the years. I have tried to make myself visible at important doings that mean a lot to others. My involvement with Tlingit and Haida, Alaska Native Brotherhood, STA and other groups gives me expression for my writing and music. Sometimes I wonder how much these groups appreciate what I do. It's not that I am looking for recognition and praise but just a little thanks now and then would be nice. The Phillip Jacob memorial service was well presented and the Jacobs family praised my reading about Phillip's life. I have made myself available for a wide variety of community events and am thankful for these opportunities as they come along.

MY LIFE A REFLECTION OF THINGS TO COME

September 23, 2002

On an Autumn day I am sifting through the threads of my life
looking for a clue to what I should do with my remaining days.
The fabric overlay spells out a pattern of uncertainty plainly facing
me.
My health silently slipping away as I sleep ever so deeply in the
occurring dream-scape.

Hoping that someday a good death will find me ready and willing to
go to the next stage.

Not in negative thinking but boldly committing myself forward with
new confidence.

Am I ever ready to not be?

So much left undone in the time remaining and others are depending
on me to make the right choices.

My will needs attention to detail for those who would want what I
will leave to them.

34%, 33%, and 33% of my stock will go to my first born and two
other children. This will be true of my SheeAtika and Sealaska stock.
Each are 100 shares. My property will come as soon as I can figure
out what my heirs want of me.

MY NEW WORLD

December 28, 2006

A new window into my world has opened at last.
I have recorded music that means something to me.
It is a journey I had very much hoped for most of my life.
I have the tools to do production long dormant.
If only I could express the happiness I feel at the moment.

My fairly ancient computer, which I put together in 2000 works!
600 megs of ram serves my 20 and 80 gigabyte hard drives.
This last week I struggled for the computer to recognize my second drive.
After a neat bit of sword play and guru help it is possible.
Listening to a CD recorded is the frosting on the cake.

It is mind boggling to realize the possibilities I have unearthed.
I have longed for creative production since 1977.
It was the year I left radio and TV and began a new life.
It is in my reach to open up my dreams that visit me.
My poetry will take up a new and wondrous attitude.

My first efforts are already underway.

It is a musical look into my dream to make a comeback.
I have steadily moved toward this moment for years.
I had to start to care about myself and life.
There is much to share about my experience of worth.

It is no secret that I have a deep love of music.
Music formed my life from early childhood.
Mother Lila and sister Sofia played the piano.
I listened intently and molded it into my life.

Their duets resonated in my mind almost daily.

My artistic side is heavily leaning toward written work.
I am trying to visit my early life and remember and write,
It is much like an ancient misty dream of uncertainty.
Picking up pieces of memory comes with difficulty.
I walk my early years over and over.

The exciting details are coming back slowly.
I walk to the Park picking up events of those times.
The sea gives me hints of where I have been.
The deep woods speak to me of good times.
It is all making sense in great ways!

MY REFLECTIONS

February 20, 2008

Using the strength I have been withholding
I meet the hidden danger that has been lurking.
More than once it came from the dark side of life.
Molding the collection of various fears came forward.
The earliest dream of dread while I was still in my crib.

Like great seaweed in deepest sea the wind sways the curtains.
I felt something strange hovering over my childhood bed.
There was a living evil, I cannot describe alive then.
Years later it visits my dreamlike state once again.
A chill runs through my bones just at the thought of it.

These earliest thoughts give a feeling of uncertainty.
Awakened during the night a cold sweat pours out.
It is as if I dare not turn around to meet this fear.
It is winter time, the time for dark thoughts,
When the blackness of night gives no answers.

I have learned to overcome this unusual life form.

So far it has done no great harm, but someday it might.
It is like a great book being written page by page.
The turns and surprises burning from a fresh source.
The urging time I must write it down in detail.

The mystery continues as I write poetry of early times.
The rhyme, meter, and musical forms come together to
Show a moment in time beating away at eventide.
What a Divine visit from brain to fingertips.
The finished product leaps forward to the page.

The elegy I play in its sadness, minor key blossoms.
Excitement as I visualize what I have done this night.
Alone with my piano talking to me of ancient times.
Way past midnight words building to something good.
Asleep in a chair I find myself in earliest morning.

The sweetest birds outside my window awaken me.
The varied thrush in its soft trill is united with
The red breasted robin's glissando to the highest note.
The evening wren is telling all of its territory.
The perfumed cedar fills the country side gloriously.

I look over the opportunities of the day carefully.
Keeping my curious eye alert for picture possibilities.
I fill the frame with the Sitka rose in brilliant red.
Rich, green detailed leaves softened with morning dew.
The soaring raven, wings outspread, lands at my feet.

The silver lure flies through the air in a large arch.
Delicate splash in the ocean shallows twists and turns.
Noticed quickly by the trout, the attack begins.
A sizeable fish fights for its life and gives it to me.
Silver, with speckled back and pink line down the sides.

Soon I am not alone on SJC rocks as others fish with me.
Our families praise our efforts that are cooked for dinner.
Grandmother saves some fish for the smokehouse that day.
My thirteenth year has its own happiness living off the land.
I learn to give to the Elders what I have caught and all smiles.

Martin R. Strand Sr.

PEACE

Billowing clouds of discontent gather on the horizon.
My small life gets smaller, less important then before.
The joy of living lessens as I try to understand what is happening.
Alone we stand, not knowing the coming future.
Ignored by some but cherished by others is where we are.

The complexity of life weaves a strange tale going nowhere.
The willingness to forgive is there, hopeful of a restart.
But who is to be forgiven?
Who is the most wronged?
What really matters, today?

Bonds that were forged in strength slipping away.
Time goes on, letting us know that time is short.
Where is the peacemaker then needed most?
Waiting for something to develop is slow and painful.
The new day shows little difference.

Longing for the richness of life again is important.
My life force suffers, ever reaching out for help.

My music tells me to be patient in a minor key.
How long away is happiness in our lives,
When will the daily tension lessen?

Putting on a happy face to those around me is getting old.
I gather in the security of keeping up an image.
Questions, pointed questions of others reveal our fate.
They are closing in on, perhaps, the real truth.
A delicate balance of what can be "aired."

In the meantime I go about my business hopefully.

I see the good around me in what I have to offer.
I will hunt my deer and catch my fish with confidence.
I will photograph beautiful images at sunrise.
And at dusk I will reflect on the good I have done.

Martin R. Strand Sr.

MY RESOLUTIONS FOR THE YEAR 2001

Looking into my life I feel the need to give my life a structure that will lead me forward

In the year I shall:

1. Collect a Classic
2. Make a donation
3. Hear live music
4. Spend more time outdoors
5. Learn a new language
6. Less TV, more books
7. Get in shape
8. Find myself
9. Make new friends
10. Love more
11. Play the piano and keyboard
12. Really <u>understand</u> music
13. Be inspired
14. Attend more poetry readings
15. Admire someone
16. Enjoy solitude
17. Learn to interpret my dreams
18. Be at peace

19. Sing!
20. Cook something Indian
21. Get to know Beethoven
22. Study Phillip Glass
23. Find my lost Tuba Music
24. Photograph Sea Mammals
25. Travel by Kayak to Kruzof
26. Try to see More with Less
27. Find Prokofiev

28. Write with Your Heart

Martin R. Strand Sr.

OPENING MY WINDOW TO LET MY SOUL FLY

January, 2006

My universe expanded to the brightness of life.
Reaching to the shooting stars lighting my way.
Our journey with willingness and confidence.
Brings us looking intently at today and tomorrow.
Creative motions and motivation are the fruit.

With the abiding help of the Past we see the reflection
Of where our dreams are leading us ever forward.
My Tribalism is the messenger of good tidings.
This meal cements the happiness you've given.
We have the Raven and Eagle sense of balance.

Your joyous work here brings us new hope and joy.
You have walked in our shoes and tasted our ways.
Your messages have stretched our thinking to
Challenge our thoughts beyond ourselves.
Saturday mornings were well spent presenting.

As a photographer I see the art of writing.

The music of words also sings its own songs.
I follow the path of music as it speaks to me.
My images are far from silent and I listen.
You have opened new inventiveness to explore.

This month I have seen the rare Yellow-shafted Flicker.
Each time I see one my spirit is lifted.
If I am lucky I see them in January and June.
I regard our visit here with the same wonder.

Marcia and I were quite moved by your visit.

Marcia Strand

PERFUME OF THE NIGHT

June 20, 2006

Opening my life once again as my computer is whole again.
Free to express my thoughts as though nothing has happened.
Going down the road of life full force, not looking to the right or left.
Reaching out into my mind for thoughts long dormant.
Realizing I have the control to write in detail about my life.

The hours of meditation I have spent getting things right
Showing that determination can overcome ignorance.
I willed my mind to look forward in the most positive way.
The expression and meter come easily with nothing in the wind.
The flight of my thoughts blend in the written page before me.

There is a calm in my attitude tonight that lifts my spirit.
I have returned to the place willing to create something good.
Nature waits for my call as the summer song of a wild bird.
Released from the trudging winter thoughts I think of summer.
I missed the flying birds in their Northern flight this year.

The music of the dark woods calls me to ponder their value.

The green leaves sparkle, dew drops in the catch light of dawn.
I am there for them and just looking is like a fresh drink of water.
Green and growing all around me I see the honey bee to the flower
and I hear the buzz of business of that sweet drink.

The open petal roses give off the life-giving perfume season.
Kissed by the faint sun of a cloud-covered day they shine.
Muted pink jumps out at you in all its glory of morning.
My gaze full of inspiration, I catch my breath in amazement.
This is what makes my life blossom in its fullness.

The yellow-shafted flicker is seen in January and June.
Near sunset I watched one on campus tilt its head looking at me.
Its cinnamon breast swayed in the wind on a small branch.
We spoke to each other in silence and appreciation of the day.
Our minds and bodies then flew away to other thoughts.

RESTLESSNESS RISING IN MY LIFE

May 28, 2007

Beginning today I rose with a confidence rarely felt.
The opening of possibilities greater than myself are felt.
The will to work again invaded my thinking and this is good.
Waiting to do something worthwhile was heavy on my mind.
Could this be the time for my new beginning?

There is so much I would like to do with my remaining time.
Oh, to print again the negatives that have been long dormant.
There is a restlessness about me that grows more powerful.
Doing something that can help others and myself is my wish.
My low energy and stiff body long for more movement.

If I could catalog my belongings in boxes to know what I have.
What is so important each day that I avoid working toward?
What is there to stop me from advancing toward my work?
It is not a question of time available for me to do the work.
It is a do-nothing mind set that gets in my way, robbing my energy.

The shorebirds are late again and I must see them soon.

They are my Spring opening to my world giving me hope.
Their lives are important to me hoping that they will last.
I have such a longing to be with them, to cheer them on.
It would be a tragedy to let them fly by unnoticed by me.

Welling up of my sadness seems to hang around my neck.
I have everything I need to get life started again.
The will to move forward leaves me thinking negatively.
I know there are people who would welcome my advancement.
I must not disappoint them any longer than necessary.

All the time I spend wallowing in self-pity is not very good.
If I could break this vicious cycle and downward spiral.
My camera calls me to get out and create the images I need.
There is black and white film to be developed lying around.
My strong need to get going might not last very long.

The tools of my life lay rusting away.
Sweeping away the thick veil of cobwebs am I.
My cameras and lenses are some of the tools.
My words take on stereotypes of where I have been.
My guns taking on stiffness in their actions.

Taking the comfort of paths familiar and easy to my thinking.
My mobility impaired by a body with less and less energy.
Hating this condition I blurt out vulgarity of the day.
Muscles struggle to do my bidding but utterly fail.
Frustration builds like a river dam ready to burst.

What are my life tools?
Beginning with my mind; next comes camera equipment.
Followed by writing and wanting to write meaningfully.
Time is the most important tool slipping away.
Will my body effort ever return to usefulness?

Three hours yesterday doing simple bike maintenance.
Bending down on my knees brought sadness to me.
If there is pain I take it easy by doing nothing.
I must take back my working ways so long asleep.
Energy is the key to any comeback I could achieve.

It took me a long time to get this way.
It will take an equal amount of time to get better.
Perhaps, there is a shortcut I could learn to do.
My attention span is brief but my dreams are strong.

Hoping to regain my previous life work is my goal.

I listen to musical suggestions of pain and sorrow, then victory.
There is always a musical message for me by listening.
It reawakens my dreams of a fruitful life ahead.
It tells me where I have been and where I am going.
The dreams are there but the reality is not.

I am taking 'baby steps' forward on my computer.
There is so much I have to learn to bring myself up to speed.
My goal of video editing is on the horizon.
Opening my life to production I know is nearby.
The urge to succeed is what I really want more than anything.

I lead a cluttered life all around me; dead bodies cover my path.
Remnants of projects remain unfinished and forgotten.
Things I wanted to do in open caskets rotting before me.
What good is grieving when you do nothing about it?
Where is inspiration when you really need it?

I have all the necessary tools before me, ready to be used.
They could spark some action to improve my life.

There are people wishing I would become productive again.
I get their messages constantly in real and subtle ways.
I want to listen to them and take the necessary action they require.

POEMS, FISHING AND RELOADING

It is nighttime and cold and no wind grieves the walls. Tonight there is a chill in the upstairs command center where I sit with my computer. I can imagine Conrad Aiken's "pigeons huddled against the wind" on a night like this outside my window. Winter is moving on like a hint of snow on the mountains making its way toward the valley below.

I missed out on the jack salmon (small coho) season because they were trapped below the bridge of Indian River long before the river rose. I fished the dam and above with no success. I have a Federal permit to take coho in fresh water in a 60 mile area of my home. There were a few large, dark coho at the dam and I hooked on and let them go. I was hoping to get the bright sea run jack salmon but my timing was bad. This week I will fish for trout in the same area with bait.

November 11th my community band played at the Centennial Building for the banquet for veterans. I recited a poem with band background about taking the glory away from war. It was well received as was the band concert that followed. The veterans are always pleased to be honored this day.

Native Awareness month started out well at the Rasmusson Student Center at SJC. I recited two poems I wrote for the occasion about the 2002 Veterans march downtown and the reasons for it. The crowd applauded my work, and I was glad. I added a little verbal drama to the occasion.

In an evening of meditation I loaded thirty-five 300 Winchester Magnum cartridges. I topped them with 150 grain Full Metal Jacket bullets. We are meat eaters and the FMJ bullets leave a small exit hole in the deer and seal saving more meat for the cook pot. The powder I use is called 4064 and I can use it in my 223, 30-06-6.5 Mauser and 300 Magnum. It is a very forgiving and strong powder with a minimum of standard deviation. I can hardly wait for tomorrow when I can sight in my gun and be ready for my first hunt of the season.

I have been nominated for president of our ANB camp #1. In the past I have been 1st Vice President and 2nd Vice President of ANB. I look at the nomination with fear at the awesome responsibility. It was a light turnout at the Monday night meeting and I was not there to defend myself. I am flattered to be nominated but I do not think I can carry the position with the amount of work it takes to run the office. I have seen many presidents get trapped into a lot of extra work and not getting enough help from the members and officers. It is sad to say, but the delegates of authority seem to be low on the list and the president means all things to all people. I would perhaps take a lesser position that was less demanding where I could help whoever becomes president. The ANB has always been a high priority in my life and shall continue to be. I just want to continue to contribute as best I can from the sidelines. This is the work of a Kaagwaantaan warrior who now is competitive in kind and caring ways. We work for the betterment of our people whom we kindly serve.

The Greater Sitka Nine Ball League is starting soon on a Thursday and I am getting offers to play on several teams. I would like to play on a team that plays smart. So many teams are so one dimensional in their goals. I want a team that practices together regularly and shows some forward growth in many ways. I teach shooters to take care of themselves on the table. If you cannot make a ball, do not leave your opponent a sure shot. This is hard for some of them to realize. NOTE: I'm not playing on the eight ball league this year because my first love is Sitka Community Band.

I had one glaring failure a few days ago. It was my wish to install a CD burner (record my own CD's) so I could back up files and edit video tapes for visual production ideas. My SCSI card does not have the necessary software to operate. I have everything but the card. The CD burner was given to me by Saki, a Coast Guard lady who was in my computer and maintenance class at University of Alaska Sitka two years ago. I just got around to hooking it up this last week. The SCSI card (pronounced skuzzy) will have to be replaced soon so I can get on with my life.

Last year about this time I bought a Marlin 30s 30-30 rifle with 4 power scope. I resized 40 cases last week and found I cut too much brass off the mouth of the cartridge. I think I can still use them with some difficulty. I think it would be better to get new cases and start over. It would be a great deer and seal gun.

It is becoming apparent that I should put together some of my poems and writing while I am still able. I have this idea of having my laser printer print out at least ten sets of the best twenty-five pages of my best writing over the years. Who would want them is still up in the air but surely some would. I would begin by telling where the work was first publicly presented and the occasion of the event. I have lots of Dog Point Fish Camp which I always treasure. I have many kinds of people I've known. I want to use a high quality paper for the project. I'm finding I have floppy disks in early Window 3.0, 3.1, DOS 3.1, 5, 6.22, Windows 05, and Windows 98. I found they are easy to convert to later operating systems. Lost are most of my 5 ¼' disks with my early works. I have boxes of printed work that can be scanned back to life. It is fascinating to see where I have been in my writing from typewriter to computer. Typing class in my senior year of high school was one of the best things I have done. 85 wpm with gusts to 110 wpm was my record. None of my work is classed as earth-shaking but there is something about Sitka history, of my life in it. The passing parade of people I knew is a strong part of it. While in Juneau in 1999 I met with Ray Thiemeyer and he gave me a list of the "Mosquito Fleet." It is the names of those who had small boats who fished in the summer after work in the Sitka area. They fished in shallow water where trollers failed to go and were successful.

Dreams of a working darkroom haunt my mind often. There is so much I need to reprint of my early photography. I have the negatives at the ready and I think soon I will use the Sheldon Jackson College darkroom to start that work. I have the chemistry necessary and the paper. There are some family things that are needing to be done. Once I have the pictures in front of me I can recall in great detail the time they were taken. My memory needs to be refreshed to where I've been with whom. I should have some samples made of the great Sitka Fire of 1966. Perhaps I would get orders from the Fire Department workers for them.

REFLECTIONS OF SHELDON JACKSON

May 7, 2000

The power of Sheldon Jackson choir rings in my memory.
The "Hallelujah Chorus" at Christmas rocked the church boldly.

We all shared our most precious events that happened there.
Mary and George Prescott taught me to speak well.
They removed the fear of facing an audience from me.
They showed me the path of good living that I cherish.
My life is so rich living in this environmental gift.

I hope to tell my grandchildren about the part you played in my life.
It is more than a reflection of affection you've given me.
I'm hoping some of my grandchildren will attend dear old "SJ".
We need to protect this blessed school from harm.
If we work together we can keep the beauty growing.

RIGHTING THE WRONG

Pleading relentlessly with my mind to get going.
I stop and reflect what was going on and reaching out.
With all my faults I suffer over and over.
The future seems so far away on a bright morning.
Letting life continue without forward motion is wrong.

Playing life's meaning stubbornly in backward motion.
I relent to all the mistakes of the past on this day.
Shostakovich seems so right in his musical thinking.
Violin and piano play a life and death struggle.
I'm somewhere in there looking for the truth.

Letting go of today is the painful part as I look out.
Relating to tomorrow is where my mind wanders.
If I had a future to look forward to, today would look good.
Perhaps writing will bring therapy to my life.
Expressing where I am now is what I seek.

Blending my past with what's to come is covered with thought.
No fear enters my thinking as to where I'm eventually going.

My life is like waves dashing continually on the shore.
It could be playful waves or perhaps some threatening.
Such is life around my struggle for the soul of the page.

SAY WHAT NEEDS TO BE SAID

Like the growling of a sea lion against the wind
My voice fades rapidly to nothingness.
Making a difference is always hard to bring about.
They hear with trusting minds those they accept.
Is there trust in my words that move?

Self-doubt hovers nearby waiting to pounce
At the slightest display of awkwardness.
I have been close to being revealed as a fool.
As I age I am less likely to stumble on my words.
I use the strength of words to avoid trouble.

Soon I am about to begin a journey to Juneau.
I will use my writing to show my worth to others.
Some day I will speak without notes in strength.
Until then I write my thoughts and taste my words.
Editing my expressions leaves little to error.

Perhaps, I can recapture lost oratory of my Tribe.
I know my mid-memory cells are less than they used to be.

The trouble of recalling important things eludes me.
I'll have to memorize important talks and I have the time.
I can look ahead and plan special occasions.

There are so many subjects to which I can bring my wisdom.
I call on my life skills to say what needs to be said.
I call on the Seasons for inspiration to speak.
I have seen beauty and can express it clearly.
The things Nature reveals give me life strengths.

I have been silent for too long.

My writing will be my legacy and not much else.
Wait, there's more than that.
My visual art prints and negatives will live.
Who will take up my musical talent?

With whom can I share my hunting skills?
To what depth can I teach outdoor survival?
Who will carry on my bird life list?

SITKA FIRE 1966

Experience in photography and the one lesson I taught myself was to be prepared for anything. I would process black and white negatives and print them in the next hour. It was thrilling for me every time.

What was my day like on January 2, 1966. I got the Sunday morning shift on the radio station because I didn't drink and could get up in the mornings. We sign on at 7 A.M. Sundays. We lived at 407 Sawmill Creek Road. I got up and had a brief breakfast, then grabbed some 8"x10" prints to look at while I worked. The weather lately had been cold and clear. 19 degrees was the temperature with a slight wind from the east.

I had my Pentax H2 on my shoulder when I left the house. Fire trucks were heading downtown and when I reached Sawmill and Lake Street, I saw the reason why. Flames in the sky were starting to build. I rushed to the radio station and signed on and gave a general fire report. Soon I was relieved from work and headed downtown. The Coliseum Theater was burning when I started taking pictures.

I had Tri-X film and I remembered doing the Tower Apartment fire in 1965 and this helped me make manual settings for my camera. 88mm 1.9 Takamar lens at 2.8 at 1/125th of a second. I also had my Mamiya C33 twin lens reflex loaded with Tri-X and the 180mm telephoto lens.

I would alternate between cameras and take time to load the 120 film which was only 12 exposures. I also had Kodachrome slide film in another camera. The wind was blowing toward Japonski Island and live sparks were carried over the water. I photographed helpless firemen who tried to get water from the frozen water hydrants. Already Franklin's Triune Building was catching fire in a big way. The fire also moved rapidly down Matsutoff Street all the way back to Jack Calvin's print shop.

The really big concern was St. Michael's Church. Heavy bright sparks were coming across the street to the Church. A line of people were taking everything that wasn't nailed down out of the Church to the Sitka Telephone Company garage behind Cathedral Apartments. First the roof started burning.

SALMON UPSTREAM

August 11, 2002

The years melted like cheese on a hot griddle.
Swiftly they moved as we lived our lives miles away.
Greeting each other through ancient eyes we sparkled.
Homesick for the mountains and water you returned.
Does anything here really change?

The air runs pure on down the mountain side.
Low hanging mists turn to the lightest rain.
The forest all dew laden breathes for the new life.
Nesting birds bring their young out at daybreak.
The eagle still sweeps low toward its prey.

Pam runs her world with renewed confidence.
Serving all for all she is worth is rewarding.
Her staff of beauties brightens each life served.
Sitka's her family and she takes good care of them.
Involved is the word to describe her life.

Ernie, with measured eye, serves the well traveled.

Looking, growing, evolving toward better service.
The tourist is tempered by the thoughtful display.
A new high volume location all helps his way.
The top five of his business line is recognized and respected.

Bruce comes here today after long gone South.
His life of service to others was known long ago.
Making things better for others has always been his way.
Good schooling and discipline paved the way for his life.
He brings a strength to us that we have waited for.

Martin, the neapolitan, grew up where he was planted.
"Everything a man could ever need is here!" his dad said.
Those words forged his future and were rewarding.
Hunting, fishing, writing, Tribal learning took up his time.
Once again playing his tuba after 40 years.

SOUTH EAST AREA REGIONAL HEALTH CENTER BUILDING

April 12, 2007

Our gathering with shades of emotions just being here.
Memories recent and deep into the past visit us.
My mother's last resting place in the quiet of night.
I come here to remember all the beauty she gave me.
Tonight I play music with sadness for those long gone.

My life journey is nearing sunset and the long sleep.
My rich full life continues with lots of loving help,
Reaching into the future one pill at a time.
The nurse smiles wide, lifting my spirit upward.
The cautious eye of the doctor reassures my way.

Singing in the stairwell recalls my history in this place.
Music bouncing off the brilliant walls finding the right key.
My bass voice echoes upward in familiar melodies.
I recall the Osorgian choir in which I was honored to take part.
The hospital had its own radio station and announcer.

Spending more time here lately I take lunch.

Tribal extensions talk to me of what's going on.
The small world of friends greet us here.
Maxine, the painless blood taker, welcomes me.
Generous portions of scrambled eggs on my dish.

There is a richness in this place that defies description.
I meet the care givers constantly in their positive spirits.
In the hall I look at the portraits over our heads.
It is a picture of commitment and confidence.

Our future looks great with all of the great help we get.

SLICES OF LIFE

August 3, 2000

Sometimes I walk too far into the day.
Powerful thoughts from the past loom heavily on my mind.
Sometimes I don't walk deeply enough into the day.
Taking small timid steps full of uncertainty, I fail.

There is so much energy spent in living life.
I take the time to live as full as I can with the time I have left.
I do not think of my time left but enjoy the present.
Beauty is a state of mind and makes living special.

Lost in the details of doing good I move on.
Positioning myself to succeed is the goal.
In my daily travels I try to move not at the expense of others.
Faintly I hear my ancient mentors urging me to listen.

Now that I have the time to write I am glad.
It directs my mind to explore and taste new thoughts.
Why did this new found freedom take so long?
I am summing up the worth of my life so late.

I caught trout this season, renewing my lifestyle.
Life-sustaining fishing nourishes my path.
Carefully I approached the river not to scare the fish.
Casting on the other side of the river, the lure worked.

I biked to the sea and found stones for my slingshot.
Swinging gracefully I let fly the shot.
Highly arched the stone, it lived for 150 yards.
It is an old Biblical hunting and sporting method even today.

A Jasmine tea moment slaked my thirst this morning.
I have tea with many friends in my life.
Sip and talk, sip and talk the morning away.
The day looks so much better and brighter.

THE SHED

My dad made the shed. I'm stretching my memory about the shed. It was for the Strand belongings. There were clam digging shovels and space for hanging deer. I remember Dad and I shot a doe out of season and had to wait in the woods until dark to hang it in the shed.

Dad's tool chest was there. It was painted blue with his name on it, John S. Strand proudly painted. His tool chest contents were stolen out at the mill when he died. It was several days after he died in 1958 when someone who worked with him brought the empty chest. I felt bad about it.

THE CANOE I PADDLED WITH MY DOG

May 14, 2000
The early life of Louis Minard as told to Martin Strand from time to time over many a fine breakfast
Sometimes I would wander far from my village to get fish.
It was an old canoe just big enough for me at the time.
In the summer I would come home late with fish near sunset.
I had more freedom than most boys at the time.

There was security with the dog at my side when landing.
It would spot deer and keep me clear of bear on shore.
I did not have the use of a gun then but I could have used one.
Ducks and geese were everywhere and it would have been good to get some.
Once in a while I would make a fire and cook fish for lunch.

I would hear the Tlingit stories at night from my grandfather.
I hoped for the day when I could bring game back with me.
It would be several years before I was given a hunting gun.
I would see some of our best hunters coming home with seal and deer.
The years could not go by fast enough for me.

At an early age I would help my Elders around the village.

Wood needed to be cut, chopped, and stacked for the week.
The smell of yellow cedar smoke was always welcome.
I practiced fire starting on my outings with different woods.
Soon I could start fires with nearly wet wood.

In a short time I would be going to Sitka to attend Sheldon Jackson.
I knew I could run fast and be good at sports.

My mind would be challenged by teachers from down South.
It was a bold step but my Elders encouraged me continue.
I would begin to form an idea about what I would do with my life.

It was not easy and I struggled to get ahead.
It took a lot of effort on my part and I thought I could make it.
Of course, I made many new friends and that was my strength.
There were also lots of Tlingit positive role models for me.
I knew I would cherish my heritage in the future.

THE LINCOLN STREET SCHOOL

The Lincoln Street School was on the crescent of the bay. A small log breakwater held the sea back. My sister, Sofia, and I would walk along the beach from Sheldon Jackson campus to school, hand in hand. We would watch the thousands of shorebirds feeding this time of year. The cry of the Old Squaw ducks was loud and continuous among those large flocks throughout the Sound. On stormy days the waves would break over the log breakwater hurling water high into the air. We would run close to the breakwater before the spray would get us. The force of the waves would be lessened with a huge blanket of sawdust from Columbia Lumber Company.

I think the first grade through eighth grades were at the school. It used to be a wooden structure and in the 50's became like it is today, cement. I was a TB baby and that delayed my starting school until I was nine years old. I was in the first grade only two days and was moved to the second because I knew my ABC's and could count to 100. Mrs. Rowe was my first grade teacher. Later in the Fall I was outside at recess when I saw a strange bird in the crab apple tree on the west side of Baranof School grounds.

I was so interested in it I immediately went to the library and looked through Birds of America and found it was a mourning dove. This was the beginning of my love of birds that carries me to today.

You might wonder what I did before I went to school. My grandparents, Ralph and Elsie Young took me aboard the "Smiles," grandpa's boat. We went to Nakawasina Bay northwest of town. I went to the fish camp at age 8 and 9. You could hardly sleep at night because of the roar of fish jumping by the thousands. It is a sound I will never hear again. Grandpa Ralph made me a spruce branch gaff with a trolling hook wound on the tip. I would wander around the edge of the water and gaff disoriented hump back salmon, then drag them to the smoke house for Grandma Elsie. Our evening meal was fish heads, tails, and backs.

There are many students from my Lincoln Street School that are still living in Sitka. We talk often about the good old days of serious learning. I mentioned Mrs. Rowe. There was also Mrs. Ramer, Miss Cleo Campbell and others. We studied hard memorizing classic passages of poetry and essays. I can still remember some of them today. In those days you had no girl friends unless you could recite poetry and play music. School came easy to me because I had the support of my Elders and family. My family has three generations of college graduates. Education was always in the forefront of our thinking.

I work in writing, poetry, music, Native politics, Sitka pool league, bird watching, hunting, fishing, and teach at the dog Point Fish Camp. I thank the two pretty ladies who invited me here to speak to you today.

THERE I GO

We all have dreams in life. The dreams we have set aside for later. The dreams we want to come true. The dreams we know will never happen in our lifetime.

My creativeness is taking a downturn. It is moving away from me at light-year speed. My usefulness to others is diminishing.

What is my immediate dream? I want to upgrade my computer for video editing. I could use sound and music and narration creatively. My options to achieve that dream are few at this time. I need space to work. My creativeness is held back with cluttered rooms becoming more cluttered. I have a germ of an idea to do something great but I do not have the space to do it. It would mean getting rid of things I have not used 10 years or longer. I fear I will have this clutter all the way to the grave. I must see some hope soon and spend the hours, weeks, months, and hopefully not years getting going.

I have a vision of what I want to achieve and the will to get started. My attention span is short and full of meaningless distractions. How often I have written this paragraph over the years. I found it in the 1970's, 80's, and 90's. It is most important that I do something soon to show that I mean business.

I miss being productive in creating worthwhile projects. I repeat that I have negatives wasting away, gathering dust and fading into uselessness. If I could take just two concentrated hours a day with them I could achieve something. I know my time is running short. My typing hands are starting to cramp after a short time writing. There is so much I need to do.

I have made the statement often, "if you don't use it, you lose it." This is in reference to my multiple talents. I have to use my talents more often so they don't slip away. I have to start taking the life I have left seriously.

My music is failing. Thank goodness for Community Band! But, I am saddened by my lack of listening to good concert music. I need to whistle great musical themes after listening to great music. I have kept up piano experiments at the SJC Yamaha piano during the week. I must start composing at the Lutheran church organ, piano, and keyboard. Playing for the tourists helps me fulfill that need. My keyboard lies neglected upstairs.

I want to present more photographs of mine to Shee Atika for their calendar. It would be an easy way to get exposure for my work. Oh! To print again. My printing paper is grossly out of date. It would only be gloomy gray with no contrast. Paper is so expensive now. 250 sheets of 8x10 would go for $125.00. Should I only think of 8x10? Should I think bigger? I have not asked these questions for years. My chemistry is old and getting older. There is some that could be OK.

These are a few of my thoughts today and possible solutions. I hope they will lift my spirit forward into some courses of action. The clock is ticking and valuable time is fading. Please make an effort to do something.

THOUGHTS

March 26, 2002

Reaching into great depths of my life I scream aloud in terror.
What does not fit gnaws away at my soul.
Bleeding words come to settle around me as if my friends.
Distastefully I try to scare them off but they just laugh at my helplessness.
A sudden gust of thought smothers my thinking too deeply.

Discordant music soothes me in ways I cannot describe.
It is so much a part of my life I can see their meter structure.
A chaotic rhythm swings and sways me in constant motion.
A strange willingness flashes through me as I hear melody.

This month I am finding out how really effective I am to others.
10th out of 11 candidates indicates my rank, as sad as it is.
What could I have done better to move up the ladder?
What forgotten tactic could I have used to be more effective?

I will not ignore the shore birds this season!
To chart their lives, our winged visitors, is my goal
Studying their markings and listening for their songs am I.

I hope they will not be as late as last year deep into May.

The sound of the beautiful grand piano told my story Sunday.
My fingers read my mind direction and artfully moved the theme.
The crowd, silently and intently listened with a lot of interest.
It was my finest hour for many, many years as I remember.

Changes are coming in my output and coming soon.
I am moving in many directions at once, lead by instinct.

Music performances are in the works and I applaud them coming.
This is the way I should be moving and rapidly that way.

Listening more intently I cover my hearing loss quite well.
Paying attention to others is my focus for the time being.
My health is quite good and free of pain and suffering.
I enjoy the quality of life that leads my path in good ways.

We are almost ready to harvest herring eggs.
First of the season fruits are so near at hand I thank the sea.
I hope I do not miss a single opportunity to take part.
This Eagle, this Kaagwaantaan, this silver guy lives on!

UNCOMMON AND LOVING IT

May 12, 2001

It seems that I will always be uncommon in a common world.
What I do is mine alone with few who really understand me.
While in Craig last month, Louis Thomson, my schoolmate
Said while we were at dinner, "There are few like you from our class."
He mentioned my writing, musical ability, and other talents.

It all has to do with my early, formative years.
I started school at 9 years old because of my TB.
My thirst for learning caught on and filled my life.
Even in that early age my strength was the arts and music.
If there was a dramatic way to express myself I did it.

Memorizing long passages of poetry put me ahead of the pack.
My peers were left behind as I advanced in the graces of expression.
My church was an ideal forum for growing positive thoughts.
My Elders and mentors set a pattern of good living ahead of me.
The many role models in my life I remember fondly.

Because of all this good will I was exposed to little racism.

Working toward excellence kept my mind busy with excitement.
Each day meant, in meaningful ways, forward progress.
Great encouragement for the good I did was appreciated by my family.
Grandmothers' and Grandfathers' approval led me onward.

My love of Nature came with the beginning of my life.
Sensitivity to the creatures has always been a part of me.
Watching the birds became a specialty I enjoy to this day.
Remembering the fur seal that no longer come here saddens me.

I would collect seagull eggs for my mother's cakes.

I hear the sea calling to me every day, bearing gifts at low tide.
The waves splash from my kayak to my face, tasting salty.
The lonely trips out for fish for my family.
The feeling of joy returning home doing my part.
In this beauty I am proud to have made it thus far.

MAUSOLEUM REVISITED

May 8, 1999

There is a lonely reverence to this place.
Little angles and youth taken way before their time.
Young men and women far from home.
Breathed their last with the dreaded diseases.

My mother, Lila severely weakened by the disease
Gave birth to me in the crisis era.
The Sanitarium was still years away.
Help seemed so distant.

I, too, was on the edge of near death as a child.
I survived the empty hours before the cure.
Loving family nearby.
Extended Tribal family in the wings pulling for me.

I was one of those saved from disaster by some miracle.
I remember the fevers,
The deep coughing into the night.
Sometimes at night I dream of those who did
not make it.

Today I feel that lonely reverence in this sad place.
I reflect on the time early in my life
When I knew I was blessed with an abundant life.
But I remember those lost here.

LISTENING INTO THE NIGHT

July 24, 2002

Serenely divided are the noises of the night. Layer upon layer they come to my ears, distorted and music like. A hint of a warning warbler call with a hint of danger to her nest, a scream.

Chromatically from high to low notes the varied thrush announces its territory boldly before the sun sets. The eagle sounds similar but with more volume for long distances.

I try to mimic their song but badly. Flowing stream all around me masks the real music of the night. But perhaps, it is accompaniment as background tempo to life itself.

Warmth surrounds me in a light wind moving in from the sea. Invisible hands reach out silently. A long lost heart bleeds memories. Gone to the world is my fate.

Looking for something lasting to take with me into the future I listen intently to the music of the night, its masked message still bright burning into my memory.

See the moon over the ridge rapidly rising, oval and orange highlighting the tree tips and glistening river. See the shadows disappear into the darkness that hides my path now.

A lonely street light is alight before me as I slowly walk away. It was just like yesterday, I walked this path not alone hand in hand in a night free from fear with hope.

Stately hemlocks rise into the darkness swaying slowly in the night
breeze reaching into infinity. An owl flickers silently across the street
light after its prey nearby.

Walking as if in a dream without direction I pass the scent of cedar.
Perfume so strong I breathe deeply. Grass tips sparkle with dew now,
on my shoe without sound.

Over to the moss garden I hesitate remembering happier moments
here.
My motorcycle parked out of sight as the night deepens, so surely.
Happy thoughts are in this place.

Growing old rapidly I see myself slipping away from useful days past.
Accepting my lot is what I do best. What if I could change my life?
What if I could make a difference?

Martin R. Strand Sr.

A KAYAK LESSON

The 35 pound Phoenix kayak brought me to Dog Point.
It was in bad need of a cleaning, especially inside.
It had a growing colony of friendly slugs and spiders.
It's hard to believe, I've had it for twelve years.
My boy and I used it on many adventures.

It's one of the most Indian things I do today.
Such silent travel with no fuel expended.
Shorebirds land on it and tilt their heads
As if to ask, "What are you doing here?"
Eagles swoop low in a curious fly by.

My boy and I would ride in huge waves on Totem Park beach.
Often I would get in and just explore islands unfamiliar.
I would go ashore and cook some fresh caught fish.
I practice campfire making as often as I can.
I always carry my survival kit fully loaded.

Night travel has special challenges and beauty.
Many animals swim at night for long distances.

I have seen their silhouettes in near darkness.
Sometimes wondering if it was deer or worse, bear.
The darkness has always been cloaked in mystery.

Tlingit spirit world figures have captured imagination
Near and far, and have their own brand of life.
Smokehouse stories around the campfire take a reality
With an elder storyteller dramatically weaving the tale.
Such was my early life at our remote fish camp.

Canoes and kayaks have many similarities.

They use paddles and energy to go forward.
One good meal and the paddler is off for the day.
The traveler usually lives off the land, in many ways.
Catching fish, hunting game, and drinking fresh water.

THIS TREE, THIS LIFE GIVING TREE

July 3, 2002

There is a large tree with many branches.
Thousands of leaves in deep green
Sway in the wind and damp in the rain.
I am one of those leaves.

Food from the earth and water travels up the roots.
All the way to the newest leaves, bright green;
All the way to the top.
The sun changes the liquid to sugar.

Nearing Fall time we turn bright colors
Before our death.
I watch the other leaves falling to the ground.
Soon it will be my turn to fly.

As I look at the richness of my life
I have no regrets as to its course.
Living as best I could, as well as I could.
Filling my days with happiness I could afford.

The heavy winds become a challenge to our life.
Older branches carry leaves to the ground with them.
Yet the tree stands tall with splintered bark.
Hints of winter are everywhere today.

Could I have done better with my life?
Have I taken good care of those closest to me?
Is there still time to make a real difference?
Questions move on quietly into the night.

TRAPPED INSIDE MYSELF

Single-mindedness races through my thinking with rancor.
Blending my losing ways in strangeness I have never seen.
Blackened again the sky is my name in white.
Rivers flowing to the south carry me along for the ride.
Stirring up sediment from the bottom blurs the image.

The sweetness of music encloses my mind's force.
Themes circular and undulation beats tell me it's alright.
Blazing fire with one match lights my way at night.
The cold is held at bay with the fire's warmth.
I dreamt that I slept through the night but did not.

A sudden chill rushes over my body and I realize morning is here.
Embers of warmth is all that's left of the fire.
My leg is lifeless from the big chill. I stand up and it is alive.
Surviving the night with the help of my thoughts.
The mind kept me going in the darkest of my travels.

So much of my life is undone and wanting direction.
The blood of uncertainty winds through my veins.

The heart beats uneven rhythm but steady.
Something is pulling me along for the ride.
I accept the journey as a butterfly in a wind storm.

A lot of living is just letting it happen in its own time.
Solutions to problems often take care of themselves.
Time is a great healer in one way or another.
My brief time seeks something meaningful of myself.
"A shining blade cuts lean," says the word warrior.

As my reason for being becomes more clear I shine.

The things I have to contribute seem so insignificant.
I must be willing to see with clearer eyes.
The darkened path reveals a thin line of light.
Is life so narrow I would fall off the journey?

VICTORY SPEECH

November 24, 2003

This thrilling election took my breath away suddenly.
Your support is surely welcomed tonight.
This office means a lot to me for many reasons.
Historically I tip my hat to my grandfather, Ralph Young.
He showed me the way to appreciate Alaska Native Brotherhood.

My grandmother, Elsie Young, worked behind the scenes
To support ANB through her connections to ANS.
She knew the machinery of service we desperately needed.
No task was too small or too large to handle.
Her vision was greater freedom for her grandchildren.

I thank Peter Nielson, Sr. in the 70s for sponsoring me.
He saw something in me I can only imagine.
I hold him in highest esteem as a Tribal uncle.
It was a good beginning for my work at ANB.
Thank you all for giving me a chance to serve.

CONCESSION SPEECH

I'm thankful for having served as Vice President to
Our President Herman Kitka this last term.
The growing experience of chairing the meetings is good.
It gave me an inside executive look at the working of ANB.
I cherish the journey you have given me in this office.

I congratulate ______ for winning this office.
I will not be going away and will support ANB always.
As an ANB member I will help on our road for Grand Camp.
The new Vice President can count on me for help I can give.
The people have spoken and I accept their voting.

THE BEGINNING SLOWLY BURNING

March 19, 2001

Let me begin with a story that turns over and over in my mind.
I see shadows evolving strangely over my life.
Painless they come forward like heavy shards of broken glass.
They seem to go through me without a scratch and are gone.
I watch them travel out into space to nothingness.

Racing thoughts as to their meaning covering my path.
Something about my future abstracts itself in mystery.
Do I win or lose seems to be part of the answer.
But it is not a winning or losing situation.
Rain clouds rapidly coming in from the sea bring a fog.

Landing huge fish on my kayak seems so impossible.
They come in without a fight. If they did fight my craft would capsize.
What kind of lure did I use to get them?
How deep into the sea did I drop my mystery lure?
They just seemed to give us their lives for my benefit.

Presents from others come in all kinds of wrappers.
Some please my eye while others reach so much deeper.

Sometimes warmth is the only bi-product to my feelings.
Friendship building has been a great part of my life.
I don't refuse the presents as not to hurt feelings of the giver.

My accepting nature spills over into other parts of my life.
Generosity of others from my Tribal extended family is special.
If only I could entertain them as they should be entertained.
It is the sadness of my life calling out in rage.
Someday, I will invite them over and my dream realized.

Dewey Skan and Dr. Walter Soboleff
Centarian Soboleff's advice "If you are of two cultures, search for the best of each and do it. "

WHERE AM I NOW?

March 19, 2001

I must work harder at my exposure to ANB.
I would love to be a delegate to Grand Camp again.
To make myself stand out from the rest is my goal.
Is what I do really appreciated by the membership?
Or is there some unacceptable part of me they see?

During the past two years I have stepped forward on my own.
I have written about friends and relatives in memorials.
I have done special writings about nostalgia of the past.
I have praised ANB and ANS many times at meetings.
I prefer to see what is good about the organizations.

Do they see what I am trying to accomplish?
Is my talent for writing not fitting into their acceptable options?
Have I not 'paid my dues' in working ways for the group?
What will it take to do meaningful things for them?
I do get some feedback from some of them that is good.

I am so new on the scene that they discount what I do.

My writing has flourished only in the past two years.
I know that it takes time to establish myself as a writer.
I hope they think what I do is something special.

My heritage is so rich with character-building people.
I want to be a reflection of what they really mean to me.
I have written much about the mystery of their lifestyle.
A lifestyle that has a ring of truth in it.
My ancestors cry out to have their story told.

I carry the story in my fragmented view of past history.
I need more names to write about that I remember in my childhood.
I will interview Tribal relatives in Craig in April.
I must widen the key to ancestral stories important to my family.
Perhaps my laptop computer can play an important part.

I have an intense desire to learn and share more about my life.
Building on my heritage in small ways is still building something.
So many Tlingit names to remember and preserve.
My work is small compared to others but I must work.
The path to the future is in my hands and mind.

WRITING WITH MEANING, WOMEN

I'm here to set you, the viewer, straight about a few things concerning Native American women in the late 1800s.

Elsie was like many Native Americans across the United States in three ways.

1. The Tlingits could not vote, own land, file mining claims, or find an un-segregated seat at the movie theater. Elsie Newell and her husband John were both born in Southeastern Alaska – Elsie in Angoon and John in Hoonah, both to Tlingit nobility.
2. Elsie saw her clan being destroyed by booze, bullets, and bacteria.
3. Elsie was born in a rich tribal tradition of her native people. She had participated in the mysticism and communal patterns of life in Southeastern Alaska.

Elsie was unlike some Native Americans across the United States in other ways.

1. Elsie's experience with missionaries on Baranof Island resulted in communal living and avoided the horrors of the negative effect of individuality visited upon Indians elsewhere.
2. Elsie came from a strong matriarchal society. She was able to use the self-esteem from her status in coping with change in a culturally different world that demanded forced separation, signifying loss of self and loss of personal meaning. Individualism becomes a negatively valued trait – the tribal community doesn't end with humankind but includes super-naturals, animal people, snows, rains, lakes, mountains, plants, etc. – members of one's community.

3. Elsie and her friends became some of the first Native people to become involved themselves in politics, business, and the education that helped improve the situation of Native people in resisting Anglo-American dominance.

Elsie may have had thoughts like this:

"This is an interesting house. Surely does look like a lot of work. How this silver does gleam and shine with attention given. I can follow duties and rules. More kinds of people come and go from this house than I have ever seen in my whole life. There is something new and exciting every day."

WHEN WILL MY LIFE RING TRUE AT LAST?

February 10, 2004

When will my life at last ring true?
The depth of waiting for it to happen comes slowly.
The inner reaches of my mind ask the question.
Lightening speed the answer evades me.
Accepting my life's direction is the task at hand.

Seeking meaning evolves in each passing day.
Reaching into my soul for the worthwhile
Takes so much of my time I tire swiftly.
Exhausted I lay panting on my death bed.
Waiting for that final moment to come.

Creative motions I follow to their conclusion.
My writing the last vestige of comfort for me.
The ringing of music in my mind composes tirelessly.
New themes and those remembered visit upon me.
Longing for a piano at the midnight hour moves me.

Clarity of motion of my stiff fingers still serves me.

The grand piano breathes a new life before me.
Wanting to play music far beyond my capacity.
Understanding more than I can play troubles me.
There is much music still running in my veins.

Life is not all music and there are other parts.
Nature calls me outdoors to search much deeper.
My kayak lies dormant waiting for me to take it up.
The dusty paddle needs attention I do not give.

The Sea beckons, calling me in midnight sleep.

Birds to be discovered are in my dreams.
My dreams reach out further than my mind dares.
Secret places remembered well up in my thoughts.
Tears of beautiful moments glaze my sleeping eyes.
When at last will my life ring true?

Martin R. Strand Sr.

MARCH INTO THE FUTURE

March 13, 2005

I can imagine how it is to work toward peace in the world.
It would take a lot of hard work and challenge.
What is Sitka doing to move in that direction?
From what I gather peace is much like music.

We have the makings of something wondrous.
Our lives mean something moving toward beauty.
Our machine is collective music bright and shining.
The language is music lighting our path.

We listen to each other and express our feelings.
Each Tuesday building into the next with expectation.
The Degree of difficulty increases and we work it out.
Each one doing his part toward the finished product.

I struggle to fit in with the group of fine musicians.
Sometimes the ancient echo of my past musical life sparkles.
A rhythm, a phrase, dance in my mind with pleasure.
Community Band confidently supporting the melody.

We are moving on rapidly in the right direction.
Composers live again on the page before us.
Our working minds again lift our spirits.
Love blossoms like the coming spring.

Every decade for 50 years the strong instant voice of family
Friend and mentor Dr. Walter Soboleff pleaded with me
"Start a Band, Martin!"
He played violin in the Sheldon Jackson Orchestra of 1922
Later played Cornet in the famous Cottage Band of 1932

He knew how enriched my life would be with music.
My Community Band answers today my question, "When at last
Will my life ring true!?"

WINTER IS FOR MEDITATION

Lengthening my days here comes and goes with each passing day.
Longingly I look lovingly and lonely up and down the street.
No sign of anyone come to cheer me in any way.
Bright eyes and laughter are nowhere in sight.
The music of the night drones on.

Wondering in silence what really has happened to me.
Loudly my mind races through all the life I've lived.
Painfully high sound beats upon my exhausted temples.
Is this the life that was supposed to be?
Lightening streaks deeply into the night.

Rachmaninov's piano concerto directs my thinking.
So sad yet so romantic, it calls upon better days.
Searching my life for some hopeful meaning,
Remembering life's highlights fading in and out.
The moon hangs large and low on the horizon tonight.

The house shakes violently in the Fall wind storm.
Hail showers bang against the roof, thousands pile up.

The sudden warmth of the night melts them by morning.
Secure, I sleep away from any danger Nature might give.
Darkened morning soon appears; life's slate is cleared.

Drinking my morning tea, my gaze drifts far away.
How would my life be if the sun shone every day?
Winter is for meditation, for upgrading the mind.
The long nights serve such a useful purpose.
I hang up my life to dry away the moisture of the day.

My life is not so hard I do not enjoy it completely.

It is a series of small victories growing larger.
The challenge of the day looms large often.
If I could make music to tell my tale.
If my expression dimension could become real again.

ZONES AND DOGS AND PRICING

January 5, 1986

Saturday, January 4th, I met Floyd Barton from Juneau. He came from Juneau for a day trip. We talked equipment. He had a Leica M2 with lenses. He's looking for a 90mm wide-field view lens. We may trade later this year.

While talking with Floyd, May Pankey came in and asked me how much she owed me for the prints of George Pankey. I panicked and gave her a price of $125.00. We'd talked bout $160.00 before Christmas. Why did I panic with this new lower price. I thought she had second thoughts. I was wrong! She actually wanted MORE PRINTS! She gave me a check for $140.00 for five 8x10's. After she made out the check, she thought she'd need two more prints. I'll have to charge her $20.00 each. I could have avoided this situation if I had let her tell me how much I had told her the prints were to be. In the beginning I told her that the Christmas special was $45.00 and at that time she figured that four prints would be $160.00. I thought I left that alone. Now I have to make seven 8x10 prints for the price of $160.00! What a waste! I've diluted my worth and may have set a standard with the customer discounting everything I sell!

Today I found that Louis Minard had a Retriever dog for hunting in the early days. Quite a find. Retrievers were extremely rare in those days. His step-father apparently brought it to Alaska from somewhere south or had it trained by himself.

Last night I printed several negatives that I found at 402 Baranof. Some were old and some only ten years old. My system using the analyzer is working well for a Zone VI facial gray. Apparently the dilution was a bit higher than last time because I used 20 seconds exposure instead of

30 seconds. Dektol 1:3 was used with water temperature at 75 degrees. This higher room temperature might have something to do with lower exposure times.

A LOOK INTO MYSELF

September 13, 2007

The shape of my life is rectangular reaching out.
Protecting my inner self in ever expanding ways.
My insights are muted and sometimes unclear.
Visionary moments come seldom to me nightly.
Dreams are warmed by an ever expanding mind.

My life force beckons to me to look deeply.
But the distractions are huge and time consuming.
I so much want to see something to its completion.
Fragments of truth have a short life span for me.
My dreams are out there waiting for the right moment.

Projects piled up into a huge confusing structure.
There are so many and my time is running out.
Energy is low and desperately wanting nourishment.
Flashes of hope come and go and I can't hold them.
Despair gathers around me knowing no completion.

My attitude is not right for the creative process.
I look to the past and look to the future often

But it is the present that presents problems.
I must use my nights and mornings thoughtfully.
The fleeting thoughts I have to catch at the moment.

There is so much that is incomplete about my life.
My dreams are moving away at light year speed.
I should challenge my memory more often than I do.
My young life is surrounded in an ancient fog.
There is so much I have missed and want to express.

I need building blocks of time to form my poetry now.
Reaching into what intellect I have is difficult for me.
I very much want to express myself in exciting ways.
When will that light turn on and give me a chance?
When will I know when it happens as inspiration?

There is so much inspiration to create inside me.
I have been reading lately with more depth than before.
I have a very wide heart reading classic poetry today.
Hardly a day passes when I go to the library to study.
I feel an historical connection to poets work before me.

The Poetry I have already done is harder to locate.
The dusty, neglected pages are turning up everywhere.
My written footprints reside also in old hard drives.
I have to get the golden shovel out to find them.
Some, unfortunately, are completely lost to me.

Trying to recall special events I wrote poetry in the past.
Taxes my memory but my pictures of the time really help.
The pictures tell the story of the times my memory failed.
I am encouraged with this additional writing tool for me.
Last week I looked over a thousand images I have taken.

I am constantly on alert for visual written images of my life.
My earliest writings were of end of the year resolutions.
I used to look at the previous year as to what I have done.
Sometimes brutal about my failings in life and business.
Also, the things that really worked out that I should repeat.

I spend a lot of time just listening to others about their lives.
It is perhaps the best thing I do in a non-judgmental way.
Their ways of adjusting to life's challenges excite my thinking.
It is my way of being a continuous student listening and learning.

I have surrounded myself with many worthwhile people.

Occasionally I express a kernel of wisdom that seems appropriate.
Since I am a memorial poet I see the good in a lot of people.
I find my work is appreciated by a wide audience in this area.
I never thought I would be writing a book about my poetic moments.
Through the efforts of others I have come around to this dream.

A LAST LETTER

Monday we will be patrolling the Herring Cove beach past the old pulp mill site. My work continues toward the dream of the "book". I'm finding work that I have long forgotten from the 70's and 80's. My early work dealt with my photography business and cultural contacts in the community. I was secretary to the Kaagwaantaan (Kogwanton) in the 80's. I also was trying to improve my business activities of those times. My earliest memorial poems dated from the late 70's when a family of three flew from Sitka to near the Grand Canyon where their plane crashed and all were lost.

I have some of the Mary Prescott monologues that she had me perform at Allen Auditorium in the 50's. "Man and the Mosquito." With her help I memorized several humorous monologues.

Looking in storage I found some of the programs where I performed Music Festival tuba solos and took first ratings. I also found several hymns that I transcribed for tuba and played at the church.

There were hunting and fishing stories of times when I went out with George Prescott in his 12 foot boat and 5 horse Seagull motor. My half-brother, John Bayshore, expert shot and hunter took me out many times where I learned to use a deer call. I took my mother Lila to Old Sitka to catch early humpies that bit a lure before they came into the streams. The school would ball up and I could cast a lure close to them and there always were some that came for it.

I'm revisiting those times and putting them into poetry. I have a list of 50 people that have impressed me sometime in my life's journey.

Each one contributing some learning experience that is with me today. There are lots of Sheldon Jackson personalities involved here along with KSEW (radio station) people.

In cultural areas I have been involved with Alaska Native Brotherhood, Tlingit & Haida Central Council, Sitka Tribes of Alaska, Shee Atitka Corporation, and Sealaska Corporation. In addition to these memories I have pictures of the principle characters over the decades. The Native dance groups from 1967 onward played a part in my life. The Sitka Native Education Program (SNEP) saw 10 years apiece for my children Sara Joy, Martina, and Martin Jr. It was worth thousands of dollars of value and learning for them. I think it gave my children a running start in their coming lives from then on.

I have a Norwegian side also. Martinus Strand brought his three sons to Sitka in the 1920's aboard the "Sofie II." John, Knute, and Kaore were my uncles. News Bulletin: On October 9th of this year the Tacoma Foundry exploded. This is the very foundry my dad, John Strand, was the youngest foreman of, at age 21. My uncle Kaore (Cory) related this story to me.

As you see I have lots of material for inspiration and I'm going to use all I can in our project. My trip to Oklahoma will be from October 20th to Halloween. After that I will be concentrating on getting a draft copy for the editor.

CONCLUSION

As you have read carefully through all the articles that Martin wrote you might have noticed the theme, sometimes so subtly hidden, of a desire to really make a difference. He raises the question about the ultimate value to his life, and of his life to his many and varied occupations or interests. He saw in his grandfather, Ralph Young not only a deep cultural awareness but also a religious purpose where God and his relation to God is ultimately of importance. Martin saw this in his grandparents and likewise sees it in himself. Faith makes a difference.

As Martin has reached back through his generations to find meaning there is the almost quiet desire to have made a difference. It is as though he has been walking through the darkness with many lights shining and just to the side he sees his shadow, occasionally on one side and then on the other, sometimes walking behind him, sometimes with him and often in front of him, but always tied to himself through his feet.

His ability to see into and through a personality to the depth of meaning, the central purpose for life for each individual and for himself was one of the outstanding things about Martin. It is this editor's hope that the reader will be able to sit back and "muse" your own way through your life so far. As Martin sought an ultimate purpose, to what purpose has the reader put his or her life? You can even sit back in the midst of beautiful music, as did Martin and let the music guide you.

Martin's purpose in life will have been achieved if the reader assimilates or develops Martin's sense of concern for other individuals, regardless of their culture, status or position, and sees them as unique persons.

TRILOGY INDEX

SELECTION	BOOK	PAGE
A FAIR CHANCE	2	160
A FAMILY HISTORY	1	4
A FERRY TRIP TO HOONAH	2	49
A FRESH NEW OUTLOOK	2	236
A KAYAK LESSON	3	170
A LAST LETTER	3	195
A LOOK INTO MYSELF	3	192
A LUNCH TO BE REMEMBERED	2	168
A NEW HOPE FOR THE YOUNG	1	78
A REMEMBERING MOMENT, PHILIP JACOBS	3	24
A SLICE OF LIFE WITH MARTIN STRAND	1	21
A TIME FOR SHARING	2	110
A VISIT TO GRANDPA NEWELL	3	85
A YEAR IN THE OCEAN OF TEARS	3	43
A YOUNG PETER SIMPSON	1	18
AASJ VICE PRESIDENT SPEAKS	2	132
ADA OKLAHOMA	2	182
AGAIN ON KAKE	2	43
AH, MUSIC	2	218
ALASKA NATIVE BROTHERHOOD & TLINGIT & HAIDA	2	27
ALASKA NATIVE BROTHERHOOD FOUNDING FATHERS	3	45
ALUMNI OF SHELDON JACKSON	2	121
AN INVITATION	3	13
ANB CHRISTMAS TIMES 1999	2	190

ANB/ANS 2005 CONVENTION	2	67
AND THE MUSIC OF HER LIFE GOES ON	3	41
ANOTHER BIRTHDAY PASSES	2	230
APRIL 19, 1999	2	29
AREAS LONG GONE	3	81
AT SEA INTO THE NIGHT	2	71
ATTIC TREASURES	3	83
AUGUST SIXTH SENSE	1	104
BEELINE FOR LAZARUS	2	76
BEN	3	1
BOATBUILDERS AWARDS	2	118
BUILDING A CAREER	1	56
BURSTING WITH PRIDE	2	114
BUZZ	3	9
CAFÉ RACER	2	162
CALL TO WORSHIP	1	71
CAMP LIFE	1	106
CANDLE IN THE DARK	2	210
CASIO KEYBOARD OPTIONS 12-07-98	2	193
CATALINA'S SHINING FACE	3	32
CATS AND BIRDS	2	183
CEMETERY REVISITED	3	11
CHARLES & MARION	1	62
CHILD'S PLAY TOO	1	44
CHRISTMAS 1998	2	155
CHRISTMAS EVE AT THE COTTAGES 2005	1	50
CHRISTMAS 2003	3	87
CLOSING ANOTHER YEAR, 2006	1	58
CLOSING OF ANOTHER YEAR	3	88
CONCESSION SPEECH	3	177

COTTAGES	1	35
DECEMBER VS. JANUARY	1	20
DENALI	3	6
DESTINY	3	90
DOG POINT FISH CAMP	1	94
DOWN BUT NOT OUT	3	96
DREAMS OF MARTIN STRAND	3	92
DREAMS OF MARTIN STRAND FOR 1999	2	187
EAGLE NEST HOUSE	2	37
EIGHTEEN GOING ON THIRTY	3	79
EMBRACE THE FLOWER FROM THE HEART	1	108
ESTHER ANDERSON	3	72
FEBRUARY 20, 2008	3	98
FILLING MY LIFE WITH HAPPINESS	3	94
FLORENCE DONNELLY	3	58
FOOTPRINTS TO THE FUTURE	2	130
FOUNDERS CLASS OF '57	2	105
FOUNDERS DAY 2006	2	17
FOUNDERS DAY 2007	2	112
FOUR ZERO TWO BARANOF	1	33
FOURTH OF JULY	2	169
FRIDAY FRIGHT NIGHT	1	99
GARY	3	7
GRASPING FOR A LITTLE TRUTH IN LIFE	3	102
GATHERING AT THE HERRING ROCK IN SPRING	2	18
GEORGE MAX	3	70
GILBERT KITKA	3	61
GLAD FOR NATURE	2	74

GRANDSONS	1	63
GRASPING THE CLIFF'S EDGE	2	149
HE ALWAYS DID HIS HOMEWORK	3	48
HONORED VETS	2	173
HOT NEWS	3	108
HOW DISTANT IS THE SNOW	1	17
HOW SWIFTLY THE DAYS	1	26
HUNTING	2	83
HUNTING LESSONS	2	98
IN CRAIG FOR T & H 2001	2	39
IN EAGLE RIVER	2	146
INDIAN RIVER BRIDGE FISHING	2	93
INFINITY	3	104
JANUARY MOURNING	2	143
JOHN AND JOYCE MAC DONALD RECEPTION	3	63
JUNEAU AT TLINGIT & HAIDA	2	31
KAAGWAANTAAN REMEMBRANCE	3	35
KAASDA HEENI YAAKW CARE TAKERS	1	69
KARL & ZARA	3	16
KAYAKER	1	92
LIFE AT THE DOG POINT HILTON	1	114
LIFE OF A PHOTOGRAPHER	3	109
LILA	3	4
LISTENING INTO THE NIGHT	3	168
LOOKING AROUND THE CORNER AM I	3	106
LOOKING AT MY LIFE FROM A DISTANCE	3	111
LOOKING TOWARDS OCTOBER	1	46
LOWER FORTY-EIGHT FAMILY	1	60
MARCH INTO THE FUTURE	2	214

MARCH INTO THE FUTURE	3	186
MARK JACOBS	3	18
MARTIN R. STRAND KAAGWAANTAAN EAGLE'S NEST HOUSE	1	54
MARTIN STRAND ON A COLD NIGHT	3	114
MARTIN STRAND SR.	1	65
MAUSOLEUM REVISITED	3	167
MEMORIAL DAY 2000	3	30
MILESTONE	3	22
MJ REMEMBERED	3	53
MONTE & HELEN	2	136
MOSS GARDEN	2	91
MUSIC JUXTAPOSITION	2	204
MUSIC OF THEIR LIVES	2	220
MUSIC TELLS ME	3	119
MUSICALLY ENHANCED	2	192
MUSICALLY RESTORED	2	213
MY END OF THE YEAR FEARLESS INVENTORY 2005	3	117
MY HOONAH	2	58
MY HOPE FOR YOU	2	128
MY LIFE TODAY	3	123
MY LIFE, A REFLECTION OF THINGS TO COME	3	125
MY LIFE'S OPEN WINDOW	2	164
MY NEW WORLD	3	126
MY NORWEGIAN SIDE	1	10
MY REFLECTION	3	121
MY REFLECTIONS	3	128
MY RESOLUTIONS FOR THE YEAR 2001	3	132
MY WORLD	2	25

NATIONAL CONFERENCE OF TRIBAL ARCHIVISTS	2	178
NATIVE AWARENESS PARADE	2	24
NEVER A LAST DAY	1	72
NEVER A LAST DAY	2	15
NEW YEAR	2	140
NINE BALL GAME	2	234
NINE BALL WISDOM	2	232
NINETY FIRST ANB GRAND CAMP	2	62
NORWEGIAN RELATIVES	2	199
NOTES ON PRELUDE	2	185
NOVEMBER MOMENT	1	84
ODE TO EFFIE HOOK	3	76
OKLAHOMA ADVENTURE	2	180
ON THE WAY TO JUNEAU	2	61
ON TO HOONAH	2	47
ONE HUNDRED AND FIFTEEN YEARS AND COUNTING	2	171
OPENING MY WINDOW TO LET MY SOUL FLY	3	134
OPPORTUNITY JUST IN TIME	1	118
OUR ANCIENT FOUR ZERO SEVEN, SAWMILL HOUSE	1	31
OUR GATHERING TODAY	3	56
OUR JOURNEY	1	74
OUR JOURNEY	2	176
OUR MAN IN JUNEAU	3	20
OUR SPIRITED LIFE	1	76
OUR SPRING CONCERT	2	221
OUR TREE CLIMBING	1	15
OVERSEEING YOUR VILLAGE	2	127
PADDLING OVER MY WORLD	2	72

PART OF MY LIFE RETURNS HOME	2	156
PAUSE FOR CONSIDERATION	2	42
PEACE	3	130
PERATROVICH DAY 2005	3	46
PERFUME OF THE NIGHT	3	136
POEMS, FISHING AND RELOADING	3	141
POOL AND RELOADING	2	226
POOL LEAGUE	2	229
PULLING THE FUTURE OUT OF MY PAST	1	128
RADIANT MORNINGS & STILL NIGHTS	1	101
RALPH'S STORY	1	1
REFLECTIONS OF SHELDON JACKSON	3	144
REFLECTIVE TIMES	2	138
RELATIONSHIP BLUES	2	216
REMEMBERING HERB	3	28
REMEMBRANCE	3	14
REPORT TO SITKA ABOUT THE T & H	2	35
RESTLESSNESS RISING IN MY LIFE	3	138
REUNION 2007	2	109
RIGHTING THE WRONG	3	145
RURAL DETERMINATION	1	80
RUTH DEMMERT	3	78
SAD DAY AT 402	2	174
SALMON UPSTREAM	3	150
SAY WHAT NEEDS TO BE SAID	3	146
SEARHC PRAYER VIGIL	2	198
SEEING MYSELF MORE CLEARLY	2	206
SEPTEMBER MORNING THOUGHT	2	69
SETTING SAIL	3	60
SHELBY	3	5
SHELDON JACKSON BOAT BUILDERS	2	120

SHELDON JACKSON HISTORY	2	107
SHELDON JACKSON THIS DAY	2	125
SHORE BIRDS	2	81
SILENCE AS NO LONGER GOLDEN	2	166
SINGING TALL ON A LOW BRANCH	2	89
SITKA FIRE 1966	3	148
SITKA HIGH WE WILL FIGHT FOR THEE	1	52
SITKA NATIVE EDUCATION PROGRAM	1	88
SITKA NATIVE EDUCATION PROGRAM TESTIMONY	1	86
SLICES OF LIFE	3	154
SOGGY MORNING IN HOONAH	2	51
SOUTHEAST AREA REGIONAL HEALTH CENTER	3	152
STILL MORE CLEARLY	2	208
STREET WARRIOR REMEMBERED	3	74
SUBSISTENCE RESPONSIBILITIES	2	78
SUMMER AND EARLY FALL OF 1995	2	152
SUN DRENCHED FRIDAY ON CAMPUS	2	123
SUNDAY WITH MUCH CHARACTER	1	112
SYMPHONY OF DEATH	2	222
SYNOPSIS	2	45
TCHAIKOVSKY'S # 6 MONDAY	2	196
TECHNICAL HAZARDS	2	202
THANKSGIVING AT THE COTTAGES	1	13
THE 2004 GRAND CAMP REPORT	2	65
THE ARRANGED MARRIAGE WE CALL GRAND CAMP	2	6
THE BATTLE	2	135
THE BEGINNING SLOWLY BURNING	3	178
THE BEST FRIEND OF MR. T	3	33

THE BIRD TAKES FLIGHT	2	33
THE BOAT RIDE OUT OF TOWN	2	158
THE CANOE I PADDLED WITH MY DOG	3	157
THE COLORFUL MAN	2	175
THE DAILY DOG POINT	1	126
THE DAY AT DOG POINT	1	124
THE DOG POINT DAILY	1	121
THE DOG POINT PAPERS	1	97
THE DREAMS OF THE ALASKA NATIVE	1	67
THE EMPTY CHAIR AT TABLE 3	3	37
THE EMPTY VESSEL	1	29
THE GRANDSON OF A FOUNDER	2	9
THE HELPING HANDS	1	24
THE JOURNEY	1	82
THE LINCOLN STREET SCHOOL	3	159
THE SALMON BAKE	2	96
THE SHED	3	156
THE SOFT GREEN OF SUMMER	1	23
THE SPIRITED CARE GIVER	3	66
THE WINDING STAIRS OF WHITMORE	2	102
THE WORLD OF LIBRARIANS	1	48
THERE I GO	3	161
THESE EARLIEST THOUGHTS	1	38
THEY ARE IN OUR MEMORY	3	68
THEY WERE LEGENDS IN THEIR TIMES	2	223
THIS TREE, THIS LIFE GIVING TREE	3	172
THOUGHTS	3	163
THURSDAY MORNING WITH DAVID & MARTIN	2	200
TIMES OF STRUGGLE	3	51

TIMES OF STRUGGLE - MARTIN LUTHER KING'S DAY	2	22
TLINGIT & HAIDA'S 70TH	2	20
TO BE A GREAT HUNTER	2	85
TO BE YOUNG IN SITKA	1	37
TO REMEMBER THE SPIRIT OF JOE	3	54
TODAY WE REMEMBER	1	42
TRAPPED INSIDE MYSELF	3	174
TYLER	3	3
UNCOMMON AND LOVING IT	3	165
VELMA BAINES	3	26
VETS	2	14
VICTORY SPEECH	3	176
VIGIL DEEP INTO THE NIGHT	2	151
VIGIL FOR VIRGIL	3	65
VISIT THE SPIRIT	2	134
WALK UP INDIAN RIVER	2	99
WE GO TO DOG POINT FISH CAMP	1	110
WEDNESDAY IN REVERSE	2	194
WHAT A RICH FULL LIFE	3	39
WHAT ANB MEANS TO ME	2	12
WHAT'S IT LIKE AT GRAND CAMP?	2	53
WHEN I MISS DOG POINT FISH CAMP	1	116
WHEN WILL MY LIFE RING TRUE AT LAST	3	184
WHERE AM I NOW?	3	180
WHERE TO, NOW	2	141
WILLIAMSON FAREWELL	3	67
WINTER IS FOR MEDITATION	3	188
WITH SUMMER WIND BLOWING	2	116
WONDROUS LIFE STYLE	1	90
WORKING FOR ANB	2	7

WRITING THE MEANING - BIRDS	2	87
WRITING WITH MEANING	1	40
WRITTEN WITH MEANING - WOMEN	3	182
ZONES AND DOGS AND PRICING	3	190